William F. Kinstler, Corporal, 469th Aero Squadron, U.S. Army
(property of Author)

THE
GREAT WAR

A Guide to The Service Records of All The World's Fighting Men and Volunteers

CHRISTINA K. SCHAEFER

To my grandfather,

Bill Kinstler

Contents

Maps and Illustrations

Preface

One day my husband and I sat down and figured out that if the U.S. veterans of the First World War were still alive, they would have to be at least 96 years old. As the U.S. entered the war almost three years after it began, most of their European contemporaries would be even older.

Sadly, for most of us, the time of asking, "What did you do in the war, Grandpa?" has passed. My grandfather was a corporal in the 469th Aero Squadron of the American Expeditionary Force. I was thirteen when he died, and most of my memories of his war stories are of the French songs he sang when he worked in the garden, and that his squadron had a white goat mascot named Billy. Now, looking through his old things, I found some photos, one of my grandfather and another American soldier, with a third man in a different uniform. On the back of the photo it said, "Guarding a German prisoner." Another photo shows a trench full of human skeletons, some skulls oddly grouped together in the foreground, forming a macabre arrangement. There are also some postcards he sent to my grandmother and a campaign medal.

WWI, known at the time as the War to End All Wars, and shortly afterward as the Great War, has passed from living memory into the history books. We now must rely on other sources to reconstruct the lives and to locate the records of those who served, fought, volunteered, were conscripted, or just happened to be in the wrong place at the right time. Their stories need to be recorded and preserved so that we can learn from their experiences and recollect their existence.

How to use this book

The first part of the book, "The History," is designed to provide some background on the organization of the military in 1914, the order of battle, how to use the records, and a general time line highlighting the most significant events, focusing on 1914 to 1918.

The second part, "The Countries," takes the combatants, country by country, and describes each country's initial involvement in the war, the military records (and naval, if applicable), and, to the greatest extent possible, where they are located. Records that have been filmed and are available worldwide through the Family History Library System of the Church of Jesus Christ of Latter-day Saints are identified by number. The film or fiche number is given in parenthesis after the record, i.e. (film 2223333), and always has seven digits. The term "ff" following a film or fiche number indicates that there is more than one reel or sheet in the series, and the Family History Library Catalog © must be consulted for the exact reel number.

Other numbers following a record give a class, fond, or record group number for the repository in which the record is located. Numbers such as these have been provided for the National Archives (U.S.), the National Archives of Canada, the Australian Archives, the Public Record Office (U.K.), the British Library, French army and naval archives, the *Bundesarchiv Abteilung Militärarchiv* (Germany), and the Foreign Ministry Archives in Tokyo.

Some countries were less than cooperative with information regarding the service records of WWI. In these instances I have provided the addresses of the most likely places to find the documents, if they still exist.

Addresses for institutions are generally given only once, in the country in which they are located. Because of the international scope of this book and the frequency with which government offices love to change their phone numbers, this information has been omitted. There is a section of Internet addresses in the Appendix.

The third part of the book, titled "Aftermath," describes casualties, records for prisoners of war (POWs), and a table showing where to locate a geographic place-name before and after the war. With the creation of the new countries of Yugoslavia and Czechoslovakia, and the partition of parts of Germany and the Austro-Hungarian Empire, it is often necessary to search the archives of several different countries for records. The greatest changes resulting from WWI were:
- The breakup of the German Empire
- The breakup of the Austro-Hungarian Empire
- The fall of the Russian Empire and the creation of the Union of Soviet Socialist Republics
- The fall of the Ottoman Empire and the creation of the Republic of Turkey
- The independence of the Republic of Ireland from Great Britain
- The creation of the countries of Czechoslovakia and Yugoslavia
- The deliberate extermination of two million Armenians in Turkey
- The deaths of over 26 million people, 1918–19, from influenza

Part Four, the "Appendix", contains a glossary of abbreviations, Internet addresses, and a select bibliography of books in English.

Acknowledgments

The following individuals and institutions have contributed greatly to my success in locating the whereabouts of original records:

In the Washington, DC area:
- ➤ Lily Waters, the Army Pentagon Library
- ➤ Harry Leiche, European Division, Library of Congress
- ➤ Levon Avodoyan and Chris Murphy, African and Middle East Division, Library of Congress
- ➤ Audrey Segui, Documentation Center, Embassy of France
- ➤ Colonel Gildenhuys, Defence Office, Embassy of the Republic of South Africa
- ➤ At the Naval Historical Center: Bernard Cavalcante, Head, Operational Archives; Jean Hort, Director, and Barbara Auman, Navy Department Library; and Jack A. Green, Naval Historical Foundation
- ➤ Jim Kelling, National Archives, College Park, Maryland
- ➤ Mrs. Lucilia Harrington, Embassy of Brazil
- ➤ Mr. Christov, Press Secretary, Embassy of the Republic of Bulgaria
- ➤ Col. Mario Oliviera Cardozo, Military Attaché, Embassy of Portugal
- ➤ Fenwick Library, George Mason University, Fairfax, Virginia
- ➤ Kennan Institute, Woodrow Wilson Center for Scholars

Elsewhere in the U.S.:
- ➤ Molly Malloy, Reference Librarian, and Carol Leadenham, Assistant Archivist, Hoover Institution on War, Revolution, and Peace, Stanford University, Stanford, California
- ➤ Barry C. Fox, Professor Emeritus, Southern Connecticut State University, New Haven, Connecticut
- ➤ John J. Slonaken, Chief, Historical Reference Branch, U.S. Army Military History Institute, Carlisle Barracks, Pennsylvania
- ➤ Darris Williams, British Reference Specialist, and Steven Blodgett, German Reference Specialist, Family History Library, Salt Lake City, Utah
- ➤ Lynn Ward, Archivist, Liberty Memorial Museum, Kansas City, Missouri
- ➤ Jackie Reid, Company of Military Historians, Westbrook, Connecticut
- ➤ W. Edward Nute, BLITZ USA office, San Rafael, California

Outside of the U.S.:
- ➤ Stella Colwell, Family Records Centre, London
- ➤ Simon Fowler, Public Record Office, Kew, Surrey
- ➤ Patricia Kennedy Grimsted, editor, *Archives in Russia: A Directory and*

Bibliographic Guide to Holdings in Moscow and Saint Petersburg (New York: M.E. Sharpe, at press), Saint Petersburg, Russia

➤ Teruaki Kawano, Military History Department, National Institute of Defense Studies, Tokyo

➤ Dr. Thomas Franke, Nidersächsisches Hauptstaatsarchiv Hannover, Germany

➤ Lt. Col. W.L. Delport, Chief of Personnel, South African National Defence Force, Pretoria

➤ Christopher B. Drinkwater, Reference, National Archives of New Zealand, Wellington

➤ The Australian Archives, Mitchell and Braddon

➤ The Australian War Memorial, Canberra

➤ Victor Emanuel Sahini, Director, Library of the Romanian Academy, Bucharest

I would also like to thank Erick and Kirsti Erickson for their help with transliteration and translation of the Russian and Romanian, and Jennifer Precht for her assistance with Japanese. Eileen Perkins, my editor, deserves a medal for her watchful eye and constant support. And especially thanks and gratitude go to my husband, Douglas Schaefer, Captain, USNR, for his research in Tokyo and for his company on several research sessions at the Library of Congress.

Part One

THE HISTORY

Watching, we hear the mad gusts tugging at the wire,
Like twitching agonies of men among its brambles.
Northward incessantly, the flickering gunnery rumbles,
Far off like a dull rumour of some other war.
　　　What are we doing here?
　　　　　　　— Wilfred Owen, *Exposure*

Status of European Powers, August 9, 1914

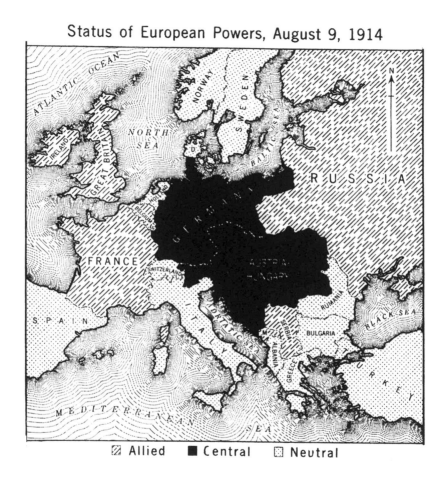

1 Pre-war Europe, 1914 (American Battle Monuments Commission)

Research Tips

The disposition of personnel files varies from country to country. Depending on privacy laws and archival practices, some military-related documents are held by a ministry of defense or specialized military archive. Other countries have deposited records for WWI in a general national repository. In a few cases, such as Great Britain, the service files are in the process of being transferred from one agency to another. As the eightieth anniversary of the Armistice passes, more and more of these records are falling into the public domain.

Organization of records
Records are organized in several ways
➤ *Nominal lists*: name lists, alphabetical by surname.
➤ *Regimental lists*: the regiment of service must be identified to begin a name search.
➤ *Locality-arranged lists*: conscription lists, draft registers, mobilization records, etc., that are arranged by a geographical area, such as a district, canton, or county.
➤ *Service numbers*: records that are arranged by an assigned identification number for each individual, or individual's file.

Keys to organization in specific countries
➤ *Australia*: service records are arranged alphabetically by *surname*.
➤ *Austria-Hungary*: officers' service records are filed alphabetically by *surname*; yearly directories of military personnel and units were published through 1918; service sheets and soldiers' returns are arranged by *unit*; conscription records are arranged alphabetically, 1869–1918.
➤ *Canada*: service records are arranged alphabetically by *surname*.
➤ *France*: personnel dossiers are indexed alphabetically by *surname* with a dossier *number*. The number can then be used to locate the file.
➤ *Germany*: to determine if any records still exist, it is important to pinpoint the *locality* where the soldier resided, or where he was believed to have enlisted.
➤ *Great Britain*: most records are organized by *regiment*. The exceptions are the Burnt (**WO 363**) and Unburnt (**WO 364**) Document Series, which comprise only about 40% of the records.
➤ *Russia*: records are arranged by *regiment*. To search in Russian archives, first identify each archive by its acronym (i.e. RGVIA); then the fond name and number; the *opis* (inventory) number; and the *delo* (file) number. Previously assigned numbers should also be noted, as many archives have

been renamed and rearranged.[1]

➢ *United States*: servicemen were not assigned service numbers until 1918. Before that time, look in draft registration alphabetically by *surname* under the county or counties where the soldier might have registered. The only exceptions are Connecticut, Massachusetts, and Rhode Island, where there is one alphabetical enrollment for the entire state.

Condition and comprehensiveness of original records

➢ *Australian Imperial Force*: original records are intact.

➢ *Austro-Hungarian KuK (Imperial and Royal) Army*: original records are intact.

➢ *Belgian Army*: some records destroyed.

➢ *British Army*: two-thirds of records for years 1914–20 were burned in 1940, soldiers and non-commissioned officers.

➢ *Bulgarian Army*: extent of original records unknown.

➢ *Canadian Expeditionary Force*: original records are intact.

➢ *French Army*: original records are intact.

➢ *German Imperial Army*: most records burned in 1945; some Prussian mobilization records on U.S. National Archives microfilm (M962), for 1866–1917; records for Bavaria, Württemberg, and Schleswig-Holstein kept separately and are intact; some records for Saxony are intact. German WWI naval records are intact.

➢ *Italian Army*: original records believed to be intact.

➢ *Japanese Army*: almost all records destroyed in Tokyo firestorms of 1945; some navy records have survived; some records in U.S. National Archives Record Group 242 on microfilm.

➢ *New Zealand Expeditionary Force*: original records are intact.

➢ *Poland*: records divided among different nations, extensiveness unknown.

➢ *Portuguese Expeditionary Force*: original records believed to be intact.

➢ *Romanian Army*: original records believed to be intact.

➢ *Russian Imperial Army*: original records believed to be intact to sometime in 1917.

➢ *Serbia and Montenegro*: many records destroyed.

➢ *South African Expeditionary Force*: original records believed to be intact.

➢ *Turkish Army*: original records exist, some records disappeared in 1918.

➢ *U.S. Army*: service records burned from 1912–56 for enlisted and from 1917–56 for officers.

---

[1]Patricia K. Grimsted, *A Handbook for Archival Research in the USSR* (Washington, DC: Woodrow Wilson Center, 1989), 156–7.

Army records: types of records that can be searched

1. *Draft or conscription registers, mobilization records, attestation papers*: records created at the time of entry into service or registry for service. Not all those who registered actually served on active duty. These papers usually do not contain any information beyond the initial recruitment. Please remember that for many European armies it was possible to purchase a deferment from military service.
2. *Service or personnel papers, dossiers, or files*: more complete record of service; may contain copies of other records, such as attestations, casualty forms, military correspondence, movements and units of service, disciplinary actions, awards received, etc.
3. *Muster rolls, unit records, field returns, operational records*: after identifying a unit of service, these records have the most complete description of where someone actually served.
4. *War diaries*: kept by units; give chronological account of action and movements.
5. *Embarkation and sailing lists*: records of troop movements organized by unit, also can reveal if certain individuals who enlisted together were transported together.
6. *Died in service*: rolls of honor, casualty reports (include missing and wounded), gold star lists, graves registration, etc.
7. *Military parish registers*: used in some European countries, contain marriages, births or baptisms of children, and deaths.
8. *Regimental returns, officers' jackets*: sometimes used to document officers' records of service.
9. *Medal lists*: useful in determining if someone participated in an engagement.
10. *Entitlement lists*: names of those who are eligible for a disability pension, financial aid, etc.
11. *Hospital registers*: individual records may be included in service files.
12. *Pension records*: applicable only after eligibility is determined.

Additional naval records that can be searched

1. *Rendezvous reports*: reports of permanent recruiting stations (U.S.), known as rendezvous, which supplied most of the sailors during WWI
2. *Ship, deck, or station logbooks*: official chronological record of events of station activity or a ship's movements when at sea, signed by the officer of the watch.
3. *Deck courts*: similar to courts-martial.
4. *Ships' histories*: published histories of a commissioned vessel, taken from annual command histories.

Army Organization

U.S. Army
Army
↓
Division
↓
Brigade
↓
Regiment
↓
Battalion (Infantry)

British Army
Army
↓
Corps
↓
Division
↓
Brigade/Battalion
↓
Company/Regiment
↓
Platoon/Squadron

German Army
Army
↓
Corps
↓
Division
↓
Brigade
↓
Regiment
↓
Battalion (Infantry)
↓
Company (Infantry)

Austro-Hungarian Army
Army
↓
Corps
↓
Division
↓
Brigade
↓
Regiment/Squadron
↓
Battalion/Battery

French Army
Army
↓
Corps
↓
Division
↓
Brigade
↓
Regiment
↓
Squadron/Battalion

Russian Army
Army
↓
Corps
↓
Division
↓
Brigade
↓
Regiment/Battery
↓
Battalion/Squadron

Time Line of Major Events of World War I

Year	Date	Event
1914	28 Jun	Archduke Francis Ferdinand of Austria and his wife Sophie are assassinated in Sarajevo
1914	25 Jul	Serbia begins mobilization
1914	26 Jul	Austria begins to mobilize troops on the Russian frontier
1914	28 Jul	Austria declares war on Serbia; British fleet begins mobilization
1914	29 Jul	Germany begins mobilization
1914	30 Jul	Russia begins mobilization
1914	1 Aug	Germany declares war on Russia; France begins mobilization
1914	2 Aug	Germany invades Luxembourg
1914	3 Aug	Germany declares war on France
1914	4 Aug	Germany declares war on Belgium and invades its borders; Great Britain declares war on Germany
1914	5 Aug	Austria declares war on Russia; Montenegro declares war on Austria
1914	9–22 Aug	The British Expeditionary Force (BEF) of 80,000 troops sails to French ports
1914	10 Aug	France declares war on Austria
1914	12 Aug	Austria invades Serbia
1914	14 Aug	Battle of Morhange, Sarreboug; 300,000 French soldiers lost

Year	Date	Event
1914	17–30 Aug	Battle of Tannenburg (eastern front); 122,000 Russian troops captured by the Germans
1914	20 Aug	Brussels falls to the Germans; the Belgian army fortifies Antwerp
1914	22 Aug	Austria declares war on Belgium
1914	23 Aug	Japan declares war on Germany
1914	25 Aug	Germans launch first Zeppelin attack of the war on Antwerp
1914	26 Aug–4 Sep	Battles of Mons (Belgium)
1914	26 Aug	Battle at Le Cateau; 8,000 BEF lost
1914	29 Aug	First Canadian forces (Princess Patricia's Canadian Light Infantry) sail for England
1914	30 Aug	First Battle of Lemburg; German forces bomb Paris
1914	5 –10 Sep	First Battle of the Marne
1914	12–18 Sep	First Battle of the Aisne
1914	22–6 Sep	First Battle of Picardy
1914	22 Sep	First British air raid on Germany
1914	1–20 Oct	The BEF is transferred from Aisne to Flanders
1914	10 Oct	Antwerp, Belgium is surrendered to the Germans
1914	11 Oct–30 Nov	Battle of Flanders (Messines, Armentières, First Yser)
1914	15–23 Oct	First Battle of Warsaw (eastern front)
1914	20 Oct	Germans retreat from Warsaw

Year	Date	Event
1914	27 Oct	First British dreadnought (battleship) *Audacious* sunk by land mines
1914	19 Oct–12 Nov	First Battle of Ypres (Langemarck, Gheluvelt, and Nonne Boschen)
1914	1 Nov	Turkey declares war on the Allies
1914	2 Nov	Russia and Serbia declare war on Turkey
1914	5 Nov	Britain and France declare war on Turkey
1914	7 Nov	Turkey declares war on Belgium
1914	16 Dec	German cruisers bombard coastal towns in England, killing 500 civilians
1915		600,000 Armenians massacred in Turkey; 500,000 Armenians deported to Syria; only 90,000 survive
1915	24 Jan	Battle of Dogger Bank (naval), off England's coast
1915	4 Feb	Germany begins unrestricted U-boat warfare around the British Isles
1915	17 Mar	Great Britain opens the Women's War Service Register
1915	18 Mar	Battle of the Dardanelles Narrows (naval)
1915	22 Apr–13 May	Second Battle of Ypres (Gravenstafel, Saint Julien, Frezenberg, Bellewaarde, Aubers, and Festubert)
1915	25 Apr	The BEF stages a landing at Gallipoli Peninsula
1915	26 Apr	Italy joins the Allies in a secret pact
1915	1 May	First U.S. merchant ship (SS *Gulflight*) torpedoed off Scilly Islands

Year	Date	Event
1915	7 May	British liner *Lusitania* sunk by German U-boat
1915	16 May–30 Jun	First Battle of Artois (Vimy Ridge)
1915	23 May	Italy declares war on Austria
1915	1 Aug	The "Fokker Scourge" begins over Douai (Belgium)
1915	5 Aug	The German 10th Army enters Warsaw
1915	6 Aug	The BEF attempts a second landing at Gallipoli Peninsula
1915	20 Aug	Italy declares war on Turkey
1915	25 Sep–8 Oct	Battle of Loos; Second Battle of Artois
1915	6 Oct	Bulgaria declares war on Serbia; Serbia invaded by Austro-German forces
1915	9 Oct	Austrians enter Belgrade (Serbia) and invade Montenegro
1915	16 Oct	Bulgaria invades Serbia; France declares war on Bulgaria
1915	19 Oct	Russia and Italy declare war on Bulgaria
1915–16	8 Dec–9 Jan	Allies evacuate Gallipoli
1916	8 Jan	First U-boat sinking off the U.S. coast (Newport, Rhode Island)
1916	25 Jan	The Montenegro national militia surrenders to the Central Powers
1916	21 Feb–18 Dec	Battle of Verdun
1916	15 May	Austrian Trentino Offensive begins
1916	31 May–1 Jun	Battle of Jutland (naval)

Year	Date	Event
1916	1 Jul–18 Nov	Battle of the Somme; 20,000 British troops die on the first day
1916	28 Aug	Italy declares war on Germany
1916	23 Sep	The "Hindenburg Line" (called Siegfried Line, or *Siegfriedstellung* by the Germans), a series of trenches, is begun on the western front
1916	20 Oct	Italy declares war on Bulgaria
1916	21 Oct	Emperor Franz Josef of Austria dies and is succeeded by his grandnephew Karl Franz Josef, Emperor Karl I
1916	6 Nov	Bucharest (Romania) falls to German forces
1916	15 Nov	The "Great French Attack" recaptures Vacherville, Poivre Hill (Hill 34), Louvemont, and Les Chambiettes
1917	11 Jan	France begins strategic bombing of industrial targets in western Germany
1917	1 Feb	Germany declares unrestricted submarine warfare
1917	17 Feb	Russian workers in Petrograd (Saint Petersburg) and Moscow riot for food
1917	11 Mar	Baghdad falls to British forces
1917	12–15 Mar	First Russian Revolution
1917	15 Mar	Tsar Nicholas of Russia abdicates
1917	16 Mar	Germans fall back to the Hindenburg Line, leaving a scorched earth behind them
1917	26 Mar	First Battle of Gaza
1917	6 Apr	The U.S. declares war on Germany

Year	Date	Event
1917	9 Apr–16 May	First Battle of Arras (Vimy, Scarpe, Arleux, and Bullecourt)
1917	16–20 Apr	Second Battle of the Aisne
1917	17–19 Apr	Second Battle of Gaza
1917	17 Apr	French armies begin to mutiny against advancing into German machine-gun fire
1917	26 May	The first Army Expeditionary Force (AEF) troops from the U.S. land in France
1917	27 May–7 Jun	French soldiers conduct mutinies in several towns
1917	7–14 Jun	Battle of Messines Ridge
1917	13 Jun	German Gotha bombers bombard London
1917	17 Jun	Portuguese Expeditionary Forces see their first action at Flanders
1917	28 Jun	14,000 U.S. Army regulars and U.S. Marines land at Saint Nazaire
1917	2 Jul	Greece declares war on the Central Powers
1917	12 Jul	Mustard gas is first used by the Germans against the British at Ypres
1917	31 Jul–18 Nov	Third Battle of Ypres (Pilckem, Langemarck, Menin Road, and Polygon Wood)
1917	21 Oct	The U.S. 1st Infantry Division joins the French line in the Lunéville sector
1917	31 Oct	Third Battle of Gaza (Beersheeba)
1917	8 Nov	Bolshevik Revolution: Red Guards take the Winter Palace and occupy the Kremlin
1917	11 Nov	First Battle of the Piave

Year	Date	Event
1917	20 Nov	British 3rd Army mount the first massed tank attack on the Hindenburg Line at Cambrai
1917	20 Nov–3 Dec	Battle of Cambrai
1917	28 Nov	Estonia declares independence
1917	2 Dec	Cease-fire begins between Russia and Germany on eastern front
1917	6 Dec	Romania negotiates a cease-fire with the Central Powers; Finland declares independence
1917	7 Dec	The U.S. declares war on Austria
1918		Turkish soldiers massacre more than 400,000 Armenians while advancing through Russia
1918	12 Jan	Latvia declares independence
1918	26 Jan	Ukraine declares independence
1918	28 Jan–15 May	Finland has a civil war
1918	31 Jan	Union of Soviet Socialist Republics (USSR) declared
1918	14 Feb	Red Army formed in the USSR
1918	16 Feb	Lithuania declares independence
1918	18 Feb	Germany resumes the war
1918	3 Mar	Preliminary Russo-German Peace of Brest-Litovsk
1918	4 Mar–5 Apr	German forces push toward Amiens
1918	5 Mar	Peace agreement between Romania and the Central Powers
1918	21 Mar–5 Apr	Second Battle of the Somme

Year	Date	Event
1918	22 Mar	German forces overrun the BEF battle zone (Somme)
1918	28 Mar	Second Battle of Arras
1918	1 Apr	Royal Air Force (RAF) established from the Royal Naval Air Service and the Royal Flying Corps
1918	9–29 Apr	Battle of the Lys (Somme)
1918	7 May	Peace of Bucharest between Romania and the Central Powers
1918	27 May–6 Jun	Third Battle of the Aisne
1918	29 May	German forces capture Soissons
1918	1 Jun	The first cases of the Spanish Flu are identified; the pandemic extends worldwide
1918	9–14 Jun	Battle of the Metz (Alsace)
1918	15–24 Jun	Second Battle of Piave
1918	15–18 Jul	Fourth Battle of Champagne
1918	15 Jul–4 Aug	Second Battle of the Marne
1918	16–17 Jul	Tsar Nicholas of Russia and his family assassinated in Ekaterinburg
1918	20 Jul	German troops recross the Marne
1918	21 Jul	French forces retake Château-Thierry
1918	22 Jul	Allies cross the Marne
1918	2 Aug	French forces reoccupy Soissons
1918	8 Aug	The BEF captures a German headquarters map of all Hindenburg Line encampments
1918	8–11 Aug	Battle of Amiens (Somme)

Year	Date	Event
1918	21–9 Aug	Second Battle of Albert (Somme)
1918	28 Aug	German forces retreat above the Aisne
1918	29 Aug	German forces begin evacuating Flanders
1918	2 Sep	Canadians attack the Drocourt-Quéant "Switch Line" and take 10,000 German POWs
1918	6 Sep	Germans evacuate Lys Salient (Flanders)
1918	12–16 Sep	Battle of Saint Mihiel (Meuse)
1918	12 Sep	Battle of the Hindenburg Line begins (Cambrai)
1918	14–25 Sep	Battle of the Vadar signals final Allied offensive
1918	19–25 Sep	Battles of Megiddo (Palestine)
1918	21 Sep	The RAF devastates the Turkish corps (Palestine) and Bulgars at Lyumnista and Kryesna Pass (Macedonia)
1918	26 Sep–11 Nov	Final Battle of Flanders
1918	29 Sep	The BEF and French attack the Hindenburg Line
1918	30 Sep	Allied-Bulgarian armistice
1918	1 Oct	Damascus falls to the British
1918	3–5 Oct	Battle of Beaurevoir Line (Somme/Cambrai)
1918	3 Oct	Tsar Ferdinand of Bulgaria abdicates in favor of his son, Boris III
1918	8–9 Oct	Second Battle of Cambrai
1918	9 Oct	Hindenburg Line broken; Canadians enter Cambrai

Year	Date	Event
1918	11 Oct	Germans withdraw to the Hunding-Brunschild line
1918	14–19 Oct	Battle of Courtrai (Flanders)
1918	16 Oct	French capture Grandpré (Aisne)
1918	17 Oct	The AEF breaks through the Kriemhilde Lines (Meuse); BEF 5th Army occupies Lille
1918	17–25 Oct	Battle of the Selle
1918	20 Oct	Germany recalls all U-boats
1918	24 Oct–4 Nov	Battle of Vittorio Veneto (Italian front)
1918	27 Oct	Austria and Germany seek armistice
1918	28 Oct	Czechoslovakia declares independence
1918	29 Oct	Yugoslavia declares independence
1918	30 Oct	Turkey surrenders to the Allies
1918	Nov	500,000 Armenians deported from Turkey to Mesopotamia: more than 400,000 die
1918	1 Nov	Serb forces liberate Belgrade and Serbia
1918	1–3 Nov	Battle of Valenciennes (Scheldt)
1918	3 Nov	Austrian armistice signed; German navy mutinies at Kiel; Albania occupied by Italian troops
1918	4 Nov	Battle of the Sombre
1918	8 Nov	Revolutionaries in Germany seize eleven major cities
1918	9 Nov	Kaiser Wilhelm of Germany abdicates during the Berlin Revolution

Year	Date	Event
1918	10 Nov	Belgians reoccupy Ghent; Canadian 3rd Army enters Mons
1918	11 Nov	German armistice signed; Emperor Karl abdicates as head of state in Austria-Hungary
1918	14 Nov	Independent Republic of Czechoslovakia officially created
1918	16 Nov	Allied armies begin to occupy Germany; Poland declares independence
1918	18 Nov	Belgians reoccupy Brussels
1918	19 Nov	Belgians reoccupy Antwerp: French reoccupy Metz
1918	21 Nov	German fleet surrenders; Belgian government reinstated
1918	13–14 Dec	Last Anglo-Turkish hostilities at Hodeida (Yemen)
1919	28 Jun	Treaty of Versailles (first of six settlements)
1920		30,000 Armenians massacred in Turkey; 80,000 flee to Syria
1922	Sep	Last 100,000 Armenians are driven from Turkey
1923	23 Aug	Last Allied occupation troops are evacuated from Constantinople

Calendar note

At this point in time the eastern countries such as Russia and Romania were still using the Old Style Calendar, which was 13 days behind the western calendar. All above dates are based on the western calendar.

Gray, Randal. *Chronicle of the First World War.* 2 Vols. (New York: Facts on File, 1990).

Mudd, Thomas R.R. *The Yanks Were There: A Chronology and Documentary of World War I, Compiled and Arranged from Official Sources* (New York: Vantage Press, 1958).

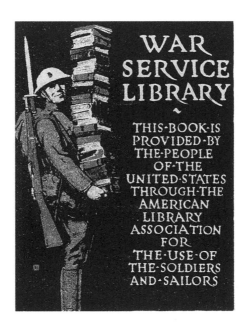

Part Two

THE COUNTRIES

I have a rendezvous with Death
At some disputed barricade,
When Spring comes back with rustling shade
And apple-blossoms fill the air —
I have a rendezvous with Death
When Spring brings back blue days and fair.
                    — Alan Seeger, *Rendezvous*

2 Sgt. Martial Jacob of the Belgian Army (Liberty Memorial Museum)

Australia and New Zealand

Australia and New Zealand were both part of the British Empire in 1914: the former a commonwealth, the latter a self-governing dominion. Australia had the highest casualty rate (over 82%) of any forces serving in WWI; the rate from New Zealand was almost 59%. The forces fought on the western front, in Palestine, and at Dardanelles, notably the engagements at Gallipoli.

Conscription

In Australia all men ages 18 to 60 were required to be enrolled in the military in times of war; however, all the recruits who fought in WWI were volunteers. New Zealand's military were also volunteers, organized from four territorial military districts. Limited conscription was introduced in 1917; most of those recruited were still volunteers.

The Australian Army, Navy, and Flying Corps

The Australian Imperial Force (AIF) provided more than 332,000 troops for service in WWI. Combined forces of Australian and New Zealand troops were known as Australia and New Zealand Army Corps (ANZACs), although the term was often used to identify any soldier from "down under." The AIF contained 60 infantry battalions, each containing four brigades.

The cavalry, known as the Light Horse, was organized into regiments. In 1917 it became the Desert Mounted Corps in three divisions, containing brigades, containing regiments. The cavalry regiments were:

Light Horse Regiments	10th West Australia
1st, 6th, 7th, 12th New South Wales	11th Queensland/ West Australia
2nd and 5th Queensland	New Zealand Mounted Rifles
3rd South Australia/Tasmania	14th and 15th Light Horse
4th and 8th Victoria	*Yeomanry Division*
9th Victoria/ South Australia	Imperial Camel Corps

The Royal Australian Navy was attached to Britain's Royal Navy during the war. In addition to destroyers and submarines, the Australian ships that served were:

Battle cruisers	*Light cruisers*	*Cruisers*
Australia	Melbourne	Pioneer
	Sydney	Psyche
	Brisbane	

Australian War Memorial, Canberra (AWM)

Military records: marriages, baptisms, and births within military units in New South Wales, 1850–1942 (film 1368199).

- Marriages and births within the Royal Army Garrison Artillery, 1888–1924
- Marriages and births within the 1ˢᵗ C.A. Brigade and the 1ˢᵗ Heavy Brigade, 1900–34
- Marriages and births within the Royal Australian Engineers, 2ⁿᵈ District Base, 1878–1939

Nominal roll of the AIF who left Australia for service abroad, 1914–18, alphabetical index (**AWM 133**)

Nominal roll for deceased members of the AIF, Australian Navy (AN), and Mesopotamian Expeditionary Force (MEF) (**AWM 136**)

Unit embarkation nominal rolls, 1914–18 (**AWM 8**)

Roll of Honour cards, Army, 1914–18 (**AWM 145**)

Roll of Honour cards, Royal Australian Navy, 1914–18 (**AWM 144**)

Official history, 1914–18, biographical cards (**AWM 140**)

Royal Australian Navy ships' logs

Australian Flying Corps war diaries and squadron records books

A Chronological Guide to Official Records in the Australian War Memorial's Collections (Canberra, ACT: The Memorial, 1993).

Bradley, Joyce. *Roll Call! A Guide to Genealogical Sources in the Australian War Memorial* (Canberra, ACT: The Memorial, 1986).

Records of War: A Guide to Military History Sources at the Australian War Memorial (Canberra, ACT: The Memorial, 1995).

Australian Archives, Australian Capital Territory Regional Office, Mitchell

The service files for the AIF are kept in this archive. The records are easier to use if a researcher knows the regiment or service number. The personnel dossiers of the more than 333,000 men and women who served in WWI are in the records of the Soldier Career Management Agency (**CA 1999**) at the Archives. Copies of the records may be purchased from the Archives. The dossiers are for:

➢ The First Australian Imperial Force
➢ Australian Flying Corps
➢ Australian Naval and Expeditionary Force
➢ Royal Australian Naval Bridging Team
➢ Australian Army Nurse Corps

The dossiers contain:

- Attestation papers (**111K JPEG**)
- Service and casualty forms (**43K JPEG**)
- Military correspondence (**43K JPEG**)

Australian Archives, National Office, Braddon
Department of Defence (**CA 46**):
* Record books of appointments, service, and discharge, 1903–31 (**A8363**)
* Ships' ledgers and crew lists, 1911–56 (**A4624**)
* Officers' record of service cards, 1911–70 (**A6769**)
* Petty officers and men, record of service cards, 1911–70 (**A6770**)
* War Gratuity forms, 1914–18 (**CP979/2**)
* Petty officers and men, punishment returns, HMA ships, 1912–59 (**A7111**)
* HMA ships' logs, 1914–18 (**AWM 35**)

Australian Imperial Forces Project, University College, Australian Defence Force Academy, Campbell
This project is a searchable database compiled from embarkation rolls and nominal rolls, and includes name, marital status, and religion; some entries have more service-related information. This information is available for a fee.

Department of Defence, Navy Office, Canberra
The personnel dossiers of officers and sailors from 1913 are held by the Navy Office.

Public Record Office, Kew, Surrey, England
Courts-martial, Australian forces, 1915–19 (**WO 93/42–5**)

Tasmanian State Archives, Hobart
* Australia Army Tasmanian Command. Record of officers' services, 1877–1922 (film 0919513).
* Port of Hobart, passenger and crew lists, 1903–51 (**P2004**)
* Port of Hobart, ship registration papers, 1873–1982 (**P1087**)

Australian War Memorial
Anzac Parade
GPO Box 345
Canberra, ACT 2601

Australian Archives
National Headquarters
216 Northbourne Avenue
Braddon, ACT 2601

Australian Capital Territory
Regional Office
WWI Personnel Records Service
Cnr Flemington Rd and Sanford St
PO Box 117
Mitchell, ACT 2911

Department of Defence
Navy Office either:
Directorate of Officers' Postings
D-3-18, *OR*
Directorate of Sailors' Postings
D-2-26
Russell Offices
Canberra ACT 2600

Archives Office of Tasmania
77 Murray Street
Hobart, Tasmania 7000

Australian Imperial Forces Project
University College
Australian Defence Force Academy
Northcott Drive
Campbell, ACT 2601

Bean. C.E.W. *The Official History of Australia in the War of 1914–1918.* 11 Vols. (Saint Lucia: University of Queensland Press, 1981–93).

Vol. 1 Story of Anzac from the outbreak of war to the end of the first phase of the Gallipoli campaign, May 4, 1915

Vol. 2 Story of Anzac from 4 May, 1915, to the evacuation of the Gallipoli Peninsula

Vol. 3 Australian Imperial force in France, 1916

Vol. 4 Australian Imperial Force in France, 1917

Vol. 5 Australian Imperial Force in France during the main German offensive, 1918

Vol. 6 Australian Imperial Force in France during the Allied offensive, 1918

Vol. 7 Australian Imperial Force in Sinai and Palestine, 1914–18

Vol. 8 Australian Flying Corps in the western and eastern theatres of war, 1914–18

Vol. 9 Royal Australian Navy, 1914–18

Vol. 10 Australians at Rabaul

Vol. 11 Australia during the war

Soldiers and Sailors, Officers and Men of the Australasian Imperial Expeditionary Forces: Died on Service. 2 Vols. (n.p., 1921, film 1439039).

New Zealand Army and Navy

The New Zealand Army Expeditionary Force (NZEF) were raised from the four military districts of Auckland, Canterbury, Otago, and Wellington. In addition to the theaters mentioned above New Zealanders also served in the Samoan Expeditionary Force sent to occupy the German Pacific colonies in 1914.

There were 16 infantry regiments and 12 cavalry, which were mounted rifles. The numbered infantry regiments were from the four military districts of Auckland, Canterbury, Otago, and Wellington. The cavalry regiments were:

Mounted Rifle Regiments
3rd Auckland
4th Waikato
11th North Auckland
1st Canterbury Yeomanry
8th South Canterbury
12th Nelson

5th Otago Hussars
7th Southland
12th Otago
2nd Wellington West Coast
6th Manawatu
9th Wellington East Coast

Support services included one brigade of artillery, the New Zealand Machine Gun Corps, and the New Zealand Cyclist Corps.

The New Zealand Division of the Royal Navy was attached to Britain's Royal Navy during the war. The battleship *New Zealand* served in the battle of the Jutland in 1915. The ships in the New Zealand division were the *Pyramus*, *Philomel*, and *Psyche*, which was transferred to Australia in 1917.

National Archives, Wellington
New Zealand Army Expeditionary Force
- Alphabetical index with ballot numbers of reservists called up by lot under Military Service Act, 1916 (film 0771497).
- New Zealand staff corps and New Zealand permanent staff officers killed in action, died of wounds etc., 1915–19 (film 0768487).
- New Zealand staff corps and permanent staff casualties, 1915–16 (film 0768487).
- Nominal roll of NZEF for WWI, 1914–19 (film 0781990 ff.).
- Nominal roll of unidentified unit, 1915 (film 0768488).
- New Zealand Army, Auckland Regiment, 2nd Battalion, list of casualties, 1916 (film 0768488). List of military personnel killed, missing, or wounded.
- NZEF. *Enlistment Rolls, etc., 1914–1918.* 10 Vols. (Wellington: Government Printer, 1914–19. Auckland: BAB Microfilming, 1988, fiche 6342571). Enlistment rolls, roll of New Zealanders enlisted in the AIF, Roll of Honour, medal roll list, 1919, NZEF Reserve list.
- *The Quarterly Arms List of the New Zealand Forces for July and December 1916.* 2 Vols. (Wellington: Marcus F. Marks, 1916, film 0449448).
- *The Great War, 1914–1918: Roll of Honour* (Wellington: W.A.G. Skinner, 1924, film 0768487).
- War diaries of units, divisions, and battalions.
- Official histories.
- Medal rolls.
- Papers of the New Zealand Army Nursing Service for WWI.
- Conscription ballots, Military Service Act of 1916.
- Records of aliens interned during WWI.
- Lands and Survey Department records of settlement of discharged soldiers.
- Treasury Archives repatriation loans to ex-soldiers.

Published casualty lists for the NZEF Reserve include:
- *Alphabetical List of Casualties in Order of Units from Aug., 1914, to Aug., 14, 1915: Killed in Action, Died of Wounds, Wounded, Missing, Died from Other Causes* (Wellington: Coulls and Culling, 1915, film 0771500).
- *List of Casualties and a Summary of Casualties in Order of Units Reported from 15th Nov., 1915, to 14th Feb., 1916: Together with Alphabetical Index, Book 3* (Wellington: Marcus F. Marks, 1916, film 0771500).

- *List of Casualties and a Summary of Casualties in Order of Units, Reported from 15th Aug., 1917, to 14th Nov., 1917: Book 10* (Wellington: Marcus F. Marks, 1918, film 0771499).
- *List of Casualties and a Summary of Casualties in Order of Units, Reported from 15th Aug., 1918 to 6th Jan., 1919: Book 14* (Wellington: Marcus F. Marks, 1919, film 0771499).
- *Roll of the Second Division of the New Zealand Expeditionary Force Reserve, 1916* (Wellington: Marcus F. Marks, 1917, film 0768489 ff.).

Ministry of Defence, Base Records, Upper Hutt

Base Records hold personnel files for discharged New Zealand Defence Force personnel from the Boer War to the present. They answer queries regarding medal entitlement, personnel files, and statements of service. Files of the deceased are handled by Personnel Archives; files of the living are handled by Personnel Enquiries.

National Archives of New Zealand
10 Mulgrave Street
P.O. Box 12-050
Thorndon, Wellington

Ministry of Defence
Personnel Archives/Enquiries
HQ NZDF
Private Bag 905
Upper Hutt

War Graves
Heritage Property Unit
Department of Internal Affairs
PO Box 805
Wellington

National Library of New Zealand
Alexander Turnbull Building
P.O. Box 1467
Wellington

Suggested Reading

The All-Australia Memorial, 1914–1918 (n.p., 1921, film 1439039).

Bean, C.E.W. *Anzac to Amiens: A Shorter History of the Australian Fighting Services in the First World War* (Canberra: Australian War Memorial, 1946).

Box, Allan. A *Soldier in the Family: A Source Book for Australian Military Genealogy, the First Fleet to the Gulf War* (Gippsland, Victoria: The Author, 1994).

Genealogical and Military Research Library (Mortdale, NSW: Genealogical and Military Reference Society, 1990).

Adam-Smith, Patsy. *The Anzacs* (Ringwood, Victoria: Penguin Books, 1978).

Bassett, Jan. *Guns and Brooches: Australian Army Nursing from the Boer War to the Gulf War* (Melbourne: Oxford University Press Australia, 1992).

Broinowski, L. *Tasmania's War Record, 1914–1918* (Hobart: Walch, 1921).

Burke, Keast. *With Horse and Morse in Mesopotamia: The Story of Anzacs in Asia* (Sydney: Australia and New Zealand Wireless Signal Squadron History Committee, 1927). Histories of the 1ˢᵗ Australian Pack Wireless Signal Troop, New Zealand Wireless Signal Troop, 1ˢᵗAustralian and New Zealand Wireless Signal Squadron, 1ˢᵗ Cavalry Divisional Signal Squadron, Light Motor Wireless Sections, Australians of "Dunsterforce" (Persia and Russia), Australian Nurses in India, Australian representatives at Bombay, and a nominal roll of all Australians who served in the Middle East.

Burton, O.E. *Silent Division: New Zealanders at the Front, 1914–1918* (Auckland: Whitcombe and Tombs, 1935).

Cowan, J. *The Maoris in the Great War* (Auckland: Whitcombe and Tombs, 1928).

Fowler, John Ernest. *Looking Backward: Being the Reminiscences of an Australian Light-Horseman on Gallipoli, and in Egypt, Sinai, Palestine and Syria, And, on Return to Civilian Life, His Travels and Experiences in Queensland, New Guinea, and Islands Adjacent Thereto* (Canberra: Roebuck, 1979).

Laffin, John. *Anzacs at War* (New York: Abelard-Schuman, 1965).

——— . *Guide to Australian Battlefields of the Western Front, 1916–1918* (Kenthurst, NSW: Kangaroo Press, 1992).

Main, Jean. "Penetrating the Barbed Wire, or How to Research a World War I Soldier." *Ancestor Searcher* 19 No. 2 (June 1996).

Regimental History of New Zealand Cyclist Corps in the Great War, 1914–1918 (Auckland: Whitcombe and Tombs, 1922).

Robson, L.L. *The First AIF: A Study of its Recruitment, 1914–1918* (Carlton, Victoria: Melbourne University Press, 1982).

Studholme, J. *New Zealand Expeditionary Force: A Record of Personal Services* . . . (Wellington: n.p., 1928).

> In late February we moved to ferry Post . . . on the eastern side of the Suez Canal . . . fatigue duties included the ferrying of transport across the Canal and back in barges winched by underwater chains. Our freights were varied; platoons of infantry, mounted men, camels, refractory mules pulling limbers, staff cars, war correspondents in green uniforms, and finally the Prince of Wales himself on a tour of inspection of the outer lines; young, only lately come of age, popular, known by all to be chafing at the ban of royal succession that prevented him from serving actively in France with his own Regiment.
>
> — Alexander Aitken, from *Gallipoli to the Somme: Recollections of a New Zealand Infantryman*

Austria-Hungary

In 1867 the dual monarchy of Austria-Hungary was formed from the Empire of Austria and the Kingdom of Hungary.

The Austro-Hungarian Empire was established in 1867 after the Seven Weeks War, or the Austro-Prussian War. In 1914 Austria was comprised of:
- *Three kingdoms*: Bohemia, Dalmatia, and Galicia
- *Two archduchies*: Lower Austria and Upper Austria
- *Six duchies*: Bukovina, Carinthia, Carniola, Salzburg, Silesia, and Styria
- *Two countships*: Görz-Gradisca and Tyrol
- *Two margraviates*: Istria and Moravia
- *One territory*: Voralberg
- *One independent city*: Trieste

Hungary contained:
- *Hungary*
- *One principality*: Transylvania
- *One province*: Croatia-Slovenia

Conscription

The forces of the Austro-Hungarian Empire were comprised of the Royal Army of Hungary and the Imperial Army of Austria, which combined as one army in times of war. At least a dozen different nationalities were loyal to the Emperor of Austria-Hungary, and conscription extended to all countries under the jurisdiction of the Empire. Regiments commonly had two to five languages represented. The peacetime strength of the armies was about 415,000; after mobilization they grew to more than 3.6 million.

Males 21 years and older were required to serve three years on active duty, followed by ten years' reserve service. After that they were assigned to the *Landstrum*: five years in the first levy, then assignment to the second levy to age 43. Volunteers with education were also accepted for one year's service.

Recruits were conscripted from 16 recruiting districts, each assigned to an army corps. The 16 districts were:

I Cracow	VII Temesvàr	XIII Agram
II Vienna	VIII Prague	XIV Innsbruck
III Graz	IX Josefstadt	XV Sarajevo
IV Budapest	X Przemysl	XVI Ragusa
V Pressburg	XI Lemburg	
VI Kaschau	XII Hermannstadt	

29

Two more districts were added in 1914, the Balkans (XIX) in 1915, two districts in 1916, and three in 1917. There are conscription lists and registers of reserves in archives throughout Austria.

- Stadtarchiv Wien (Vienna City Archives). Stellunglisten (draft lists), 1820–1914.
- Steyr Oberösterreich Bezirkshauptmannschaft. Stellungslisten der Militärp-flichtigen, 1865–1918 (film 1921089 ff.). Conscription lists, register of military tax records, and register of those in military reserves. The records are at the Oberösterreichischen Landesarchiv in Linz.

The Army and Navy

The term "KuK" stood for *Kaiserlich und Königlich*, Imperial and Royal, the name for the common army and navy. The *Landwehr* (*Honvéd* in Hungary) were the territorial armies responsible for home defense. Reserve troops were mobilized from the *Landsturm*.

After mobilization the Imperial Army had 102 infantry regiments, the Austrian *Landwehr* 38, and the Hungarian *Honvéd* 32; 60 cavalry regiments; 82 artillery regiments; the engineer, signal, and railway corps, and the *Luftfahrttuppen* (Flying Corps).

➤ *Stellunglisten*: draft lists, includes birthdate of soldier and parents' names
➤ *Qualifikationlisten*: officers' service records
➤ *Musterlisten*: muster rolls
➤ *Gründbuchblatter*: foundation books which provide information on officers and soldiers, with a service sheet for each soldier
➤ *Abangsprotokolle*: discharge records
➤ *Pensionsprotokolle*: military pension records
➤ *Heriatskautionen*: officers' marriages

Österreichisches Staatsarchiv, Kriegsarchiv, Vienna

Austro-Hungarian Imperial Army

- Army service sheets, 1820–1918
- Army enlistment registers and enrollment lists, 1862–1918
- Soldiers' returns, 1918–20
- Military unit records, 1914–18
- Pensionsprotokolle 1773–1920 (film 1353183 ff.). Military pension records for officers, officials, employees, and military widows and orphans, and some enlisted.
- Dienstbeschreibungen und qualifikationlisten der offiziere, 1823–1918 (film 1187917 ff.). Service records for officers and military officials of the army

of the Austro-Hungarian Empire, alphabetically arranged.

- Gründbuchblatter, 1869–1918
- Hospital death registers, 1779–1922
- Military parish registers for the Austro-Hungarian Empire
- Militär-Matriken index, 1740–1922 (film 1442862 ff.). Card index of regiments, hospitals, and place-names in military parish registers of the Austro-Hungarian Empire.
- Prisoner of war card index, 1914–18
- Heriatskautionen (officers' marriages), 1750–1918, arranged chronologically

Evidenzent de Kriegsmarine (Imperial navy)

- Gründbuchblatter, 1760–1918
- Qualificationlisten, 1869–1928
- Assenprtokolle, 1869–1918
- Kasperkovitz, Otto. *Diskokations-Verzeichnis des KuK Heeres und der KuK Marine* (Vienna: The Kriegsarchiv, 1969, film 1186632). Distribution location index of the Austro-Hungarian Empire army and navy troops, regiments, battalions, etc.

Hadtörténelmi Levéltár, Budapest
The Archives of Military History holds the operation records for *Honvéd* headquarters, 1869–1918, including some information on individual soldiers.

Magyar Oszágos Levéltár, Budapest
The National Archives of Hungary holds military conscription registers through 1918.

Österreich Staatsarchiv
Abteling IV
Kriegsarchiv
Nottendorfergasse 2-4
1030 Vienna

Archives of Military History
Hadtörténelmi Levéltar
Kapisztrán tér 2
1250 Budapest

Military History Museum
Heersgeschichtliches Museum
Ghentgastresse Objekt 18
1030 Vienna

Hungarian State Archives
Magyar Oszágos Levéltár
Bécsi Kapu tér 4
1250 Budapest

Austrian National Library
Österreichishe Nationalbibliothek
Josefplatz 1
Postfach 308
1015 Vienna

Budapest History Museum
Budapesti Történeti Múzeum
Szent György tér 2
1014 Budapest

The yearly directories of military personnel and units of the Imperial Austrian Army have been published in *Militär-Schematismus des Österreichischen Kaiserthumes* (Vienna: Aus der K.K. Hof-und Staatsdruckerei, 1790–1918, film 1506188 ff.). Included are:

➢ Östreichischer Miliz-Almanach
➢ Kais Königl. Militär-Schematismus
➢ Schematismus für das KuK Heer und für die KuK Kriegs-Marine
➢ Ranglisten des KuK Heeres
➢ Ranglisten der kk Landwehr und der kk Gendarmerie

The Crown Lands of Austria-Hungary

After the war, many parts of the Empire were ceded to the new states of Yugoslavia and Czechoslovakia. Today some of them are independent republics. If military service was rendered in the Imperial army, the records would still be at the *Kriegsarchiv* in Vienna. Regional and state archives also have historical collections that may contain additional information. To see the post-war disposition of localities not listed below, please see the section entitled "Aftermath."

Banat

Horváth, Eugene. *The Banat: A Forgotten Chapter of European History* (Budapest: Sárkány Printing Co., 1931, film 1344049). A history of the Banat region of Hungary, now called Vojvodina, Serbia.

Schmidt, Josef. *Die Banater Kirchenbücher: Eine Bestandsaufnahme der verfilmten Banater Kirchenbücher in der Bibliothek des Instituts für Auslandsbeziehungen* (Stuttgart: Bibliothek und Dokumentationsstelle des Instituts, 1979). An inventory of the microfilmed Banat parish registers in the Library of the *Institut für Auslandsbeziehungen*, Stuttgart. The Banat area of Austria-Hungary was later divided among Yugoslavia, Romania, and Hungary.

Bosnia and Herzegovina

Archives and monuments in this area were severely and sometimes deliberately damaged or destroyed by Serb forces from 1992 to 1995, particularly the National Library.

National Museum of Bosnia and Herzegovina
Zemaljski Muzej BiH
Zmaja od Bosne 7
71000 Sarajevo

National and University Library of Bosnia and Herzegovina
Narodna i univerzitetska biblioteka Bosne i Hercegovine
OPB 337
Obala Vojvode Stepe 42
71000 Sarajevo

Donia R. *Islam under the Double Eagle: The Muslims of Bosnia and Herzegovina, 1878-1914* (Boulder, CO: Eastern European Monographs, 1981).

Croatia
Eterovich, Francis H. *Croatia: Land, People, Culture.* 2 Vols. (Toronto: University of Toronto Press, 1969-70).

Records in the Croatian State Archives, Zagreb
- Österreich Armee Feldspital 13. Kirchenbuch, 1914-18 (film 1921772 ff.). Military hospital registers of deaths for Austrian regiments.
- Österreich Armee. Spital Ópázua, Slavonien. Kirchenbuch, 1915-18 (film 1921770 ff.). Military hospital parish registers of deaths for Ópázua, Slavonien, Austria, also called Ópazova, Szerém, Hungary, now Stara Pazova, Serbia.

Croatian State Archives
Hvratski državni arhiv
Marulićev trg 21
10000 Zagreb

Historical Museum of Croatia
Hvratski povijesni muzej
Matoševa 9
10000 Zagreb

Czechoslovakia (Bohemia, Moravia, Ruthenia, Slovakia)
Czech military service during WWI was not confined to the Austro-Hungarian Army. A volunteer army, *Ceská Družina,* was formed in August 1914 by leaders of the Czech colony in Russia, including deserters from the Imperial army and 100,000 Czech citizens of the Russian Empire. The Czech Foreign Committee was formed in exile in Paris in November 1915 to work for Czech independence. After the abdication of the Russian Tsar in 1917, the *Družina,* known as the Czech Legion, fought for Russia on the eastern front in July 1917. Caught in the Russian Revolution of 1918, the Legion was unable to leave Russia. They fought in defense of the newly declared Siberian Republic in August 1918, along with contingents from the U.S., Great Britain, Japan, and the White Russians.

The Czech Legion was marooned in Siberia after the Armistice, and the Siberian government crumbled in 1919. The Legion then fought its way to Vladivostok, where the troops were evacuated by Red Cross and private Czech-American ships. They were transported to San Francisco, and were then able to return home to their new country of Czechoslovakia, which included Slovakia, Moravia, Bohemia, Ruthenia, and part of Silesia.

Slovaks also fought with the Russian army, although Hungary made it more difficult for them to desert from the Austro-Hungarian army.

Czech National Library
Národní knihovna Česke Republiky
Klementinum 190
110 01 Prague

Czech Republic Central Military Library
Ústřední vojenská knihovna
Rooseveltova 23
160 00 Prague

Slovak National Library
Slovenská národnákniznica v
Matici slovenskej
Novomeského 32
03652 Martin

Slovak National Museum
Slovenské národné múzeum
Vajanského nábr. 2
814 36 Bratislava

Hoyt, Edwin P. *The Army Without a Country* (New York: Macmillan, 1967).

Seton-Watson, R.W. *History of the Czechs and the Slovaks* (London: Hutchinson, 1943).

Unterberger, Betty. *The United States, Revolutionary Russia, and the Rise of Czechoslovakia* (Chapel Hill: University of North Carolina Press, 1989).

Galicia
Magocsi, Paul Robert. *Galicia: A Historical Survey and Bibliographic Guide* (Toronto: University of Toronto Press, 1983). History of Galicians in Austria, Poland, and the Ukraine.

Slavonia
Hadjetz-Loeber, Irmgard. *Heimatbuch Neu-Pasua. Die Geschichte eines donauschwäbischen Dorfes* (Stuttgart: Heimatausschusses von Neu Pasua, 1956, film 1270130). History of Neu Pasua, Syrmia, Slavonia, Austria, also called Ujpazova, Szerém, Hungary, now Nova Pazova, Serbia, Yugoslavia.

Slovenia

Archives of the Republic of
Slovenia
Arhiv Republike Slovenije
Zvezdarska 1
1000 Ljubljana

National and University Library
Ljublana
POB 259
Turjaska 1
1001 Ljubljana

Transylvania

Transylvania was home to two million Hungarians (Magyars) and more than three million ethnic Romanians, who suffered cultural persecution from the Hungarian government. They, like the rest of Austria-Hungary, were liable for conscription in the Imperial army. After the war, Romania annexed Transylvania.

Pascu, Stefan. *A History of Transylvania* (Detroit: Wayne State University Press, 1982).

Archival Guides

Arhive Hrvatske. *Inventar zbirke maticnih knijga roenih, vjencanih i umrlih* (n.p., 1970, film 1184080). Inventory of vital records of Croatia, Yugoslavia. Includes Roman Catholic, Greek Orthodox, Russian Orthodox, Jewish, military, Reformed Church records, and transcripts.

Balázs, Pétwe. *Guide to the Archives of Hungary* (Budapest: Archival Board of the Ministry of Culture, 1976, film 1183502).

Der Voralberger Landesarchiv: Einführung und Bestandsübersicht (Bregenz: n.p., 1969, fiche 6001501). Holdings of the Voralberger Lanadesarchiv in Bregenz, Austria.

Egger, Rainer. *The Kriegsarchiv* (Houston, TX: Rice University, 1971, fiche 6001424). The Vienna War Archives collection of military records for the former Austrian Empire.

Kajdoš, Vladimír. *Průvodce po archiních fondech okresního archivu ve Frenštáště pod Radhoštěm* (Frenštáště pod Radhoštěm: Okresní Národní Výbor, 1959, film 1183615). Holdings of the district archive in Frenštáště pod Radhoštěm, Morava, Czech Republic (formerly Frankstadt, Mähren, Austria).

Nemeth, Kresimir. *Using the Croatian Archives for Genealogical Research and Family History* (Salt Lake City: Corporation of the President, 1980, fiche 6085783).

Posch, Fritz. *Gasamtinventar des Steiermärkischen Landesarchives* (Graz: The Archive, 1959, fiche 6001422). Holdings of the Steiermärk Lanadesarchiv in Graz, Austria.

Vjesnik historijskih arhiva u Rijeci i Pazinu (Rijeka: n.p., 1969, film 1045486). Historical almanac of archives in Rijeka and Pazin, Yugoslavia. Includes holdings of the archive in Mosćenicje, Croatia.

Vjesnik Kr. *Hrvatsko-Slavonsko-Dalmatinskoga zemaljskog arkiva* (Zagreb: Kralj. zemaljske tiskare, 1916, film 1181596). Journal of the archives of the Kingdom of Croatia-Slavonia-Dalmatia.

Vodnik po zupnijskih arhivih na Obmocju SR Slovenije. 2 Vols. (Ljubljana: Izdala Skupnost Arhivov Slovenije, 1975). Inventory of records other than parish registers in church archives in Slovenia, formerly in the provinces of Krain, Steiermark, and Küstenland, Austria.

Volf, Miloslav. *Popis Městských v Čechách* (Prague: Nákladem Zemského Náodního Výboru, 1947, film 0908536). Holdings of city archives in Cěchy (Bohemia).

Suggested Reading

Blodgett, Steven W. *Great-Grandfather Was in the Imperial Cavalry: Using Austrian Military Records as an Aid to Writing Family History* (Salt Lake City: Corporation of the President, 1980, fiche 6085770).

Hoensch, Jörg K. *A History of Modern Hungary* (New York: Longman, 1988).

Lucas, J.S. *Austro-Hungarian Infantry, 1914–1918* (London: Almark, 1973).

Molnár, Éva. *Hungary: Essential Facts, Figures, and Pictures* (Budapest: MTI Media Data Bank, 1995).

Seton-Watson, R.W. *Sarajevo: A Study in the Origins of the Great War* (London: Hutchinson, 1926).

Taylor, A.J.P. *The Hapsburg Monarchy, 1915–1918* (London: Hamish Hamilton, 1944).

Belgium

German troops invaded Belgium on 4 August 1914. The Belgians fought bravely, but their small army was no match for the 300,000 invading German troops. Liège was the first to fall, forcing the Belgian army to retreat to the Fortress at Antwerp. German troops occupied Brussels on 20 August. After the Battle of the Marne, the Germans laid siege to Antwerp on 28 September. Led by King Albert, the Belgians abandoned the city on 6 October and fell back to the Yser. During the Battle of Ypres, casualties were very heavy on both sides, but the Belgian army escaped at Nieuport.

The army remained at Yser for four years while Belgium was occupied. During the German occupation some 120,000 Belgians were deported to Germany to serve as forced labor. In September 1918 King Albert led the Flanders Army Corps — comprised of British, French, and Belgian troops — in the final Allied offensive to retake Belgium.

Conscription

In Belgium the policy in 1914 stated that single males age 20 were liable for 15 months' active service with a regiment (longer with field artillery or horse artillery). Married men were only required to perform four months' service. The *Gendarmerie* (cavalry) was made up of 3,000 men, and the *Carde Civique*, similar to a national guard, drilled ten times a year. Conscription registration was done by canton, and the records that have survived remain in local archives. The six infantry regiments were recruited from Antwerp, Brussels, Ghent, Liège, Mons, and Namur. One cavalry unit was based in Brussels; there was a mobile brigade in Namur and another in Liège, and 11 air squadrons. After mobilization total Belgian forces numbered 117,000.

The Army

During the war, when Belgium was occupied by Germany, army training was conducted in France. Belgian hospitals were opened in France and England. The air squadron, *Aviation Militaire*, conducted fighter and bombing missions in 1915. Belgian troops also fought in the Belgian Congo and with British forces against German East Africa.

Gendarmerie, Brussels

Personnel records for WWI are kept here; it is helpful to know the regiment of service.

Musée Royal de l'Armée et d'Histoire Militaire, Brussels
The library of the Museum has a large collection of regimental histories, diaries, operational records, and published works.

Guide Musée Royal de l'Armée et d'Histoire Militaire (Brussels: The Museum, 1984). Guide to the Royal Museum of Military History in Belgium.

Gendarmie	***Musée Royal de l'Armée et***
Centre de documentaion	***d'Histoire Militaire***
Rue Fritz Toussiant 47	Bibliothèque
1050 Brussels	Palais du Conquantenaire 3
	1040 Brussels

Hoover Institution, Stanford University, Stanford, California
* Belgian subject collection
* Belgian Territory (German occupation) issuances, 1914–18
* Letters from Belgian soldiers in France, 1917–20

Suggested Reading
Buffin, Baron C. *Brave Belgium* (New York: P.G. Putnam's Sons, 1918).

Haag, Henri, et al. *Histoire de la Belgique Contemporaire, 1914–1970* (Brussels: La Renaissance du Livre, 1975).

Heuvel, J. van der. *Slave Raids in Belgium: The Facts about the Deportations* (London: Fisher Unwin, 1917).

Overtraeten, General R. van. *The War Diaries of Albert I, King of the Belgians* (London: William Kimber, 1954).

Terlinden, Charles. *Histoire Militaire des Belges*. 2 Vols. (Brussels: La Renaissance du Livre, 1969).

Tuchman, Barbara. *The Guns of August* (New York: Macmillan, 1962).

Twells, J.H. *In the Prison City: Brussels, 1914–1918* (London: Melrose, 1919).

Brazil

Brazil was the only South American country to commit troops for service in WWI. On 4 April 1917 the Brazilian steamer *Paraná* was sunk by a U-boat off Cherbourg, followed by other sinkings in May and October. Brazil declared war on Germany on 26 October 1917.

Conscription

Males ages 21 to 44 were liable for two years' active army service, followed by seven years in the first levy of the reserve, then seven more in the second levy, and finally eight years in the national guard. When Brazil entered the war, males ages 21 to 30 were called up for active service.

The Army and Navy

Brazilian army troops served as support troops and on the western front. The Brazilian navy served in the Atlantic, the largest capital ships being the dreadnoughts *Minas Geraes* and *São Paolo*.

Biblioteca do Exército, Brasília

Normas para a preservasão das tradições Militares do Exército Brasiliero (Brasilia: Ministério do Ezército, 1987). Organization charts and pedigrees of Brazilian army units.

National Library
Biblioteca Nacional
Av. Rio Branco 219-39
Rio de Janeiro, RJ
20042

National Archives of Brazil
Archivo Nacional do Brasil
R. Azeredo Coutinho 77
Rio de Janeiro, RJ
20230

Suggested Reading

Albert, Bill. *South America and the First World War* (Cambridge: Cambridge University Press, 1988).

Barroso, Gustavo. *História militar do Brasil* (Sao Paulo: Companhia Editora Nacional, 1935, film 0962400). Military history of Brazil.

Kirkpatrick, F.A. *South America and the War* (London: CUP, 1918).

3 Austrian army medic (Liberty Memorial Museum)

Bulgaria

Bulgaria did not enter WWI until September 1915, on the side of the Central Powers. On 16 October the Bulgarian army invaded Serbia. Greece, which was bound by treaty to come to Serbia's aid, did nothing but ask for military assistance from France and England. British and French troops landed at Salonika (Greece) on 5 October. On 22 October, while negotiations were being conducted by the French and British on how to proceed with the campaign, the Bulgarians cut off any possibility of the Allied forces reaching the Serbian army. The Bulgarian army went on to occupy portions of northern Greece and to participate in the attack on Romania in 1916.

Germany's constant drain on Bulgarian resources left Bulgaria in shaky condition. In September 1918 Allied troops invaded Bulgaria. Bulgaria signed an armistice at the end of the month and withdrew from all occupied territories.

Conscription
Males from age 21 were liable for two years' active service in the *deistvuyushta armia*, followed by eight years in the first levy of the reserve, then seven years in the second levy, and finally service in the territorial *narodon opolchie* until age 46.

The Army
The Bulgarian army benefitted from training with the Russian army. The army was formed into nine divisions, which formed three field armies. The divisions were headquartered in:

Sofia	Plevna	Sliven
Dupnitza	Rustchuk	Stara-Zagora
Philipopolis	Shumla	Vratza

National Library of Saint Cyrill and Saint Methodius
Naronda Biblioteka Sv. Sv. Kiril i
    Metodii
blvd Vassel Levski 88
1504 Sofia

Director General of Archives
Glavno Upravlenie na Archivite
Moskozska 5
1000 Sofia

Suggested Reading
Crampton, R.J. *Bulgaria, 1878–1918: A History* (Boulder, CO: Eastern European Quarterly, 1983).

Vlahov, Tushe. *Otnosheniya mezdu Bŭlgariya i Tsenralnite sili prez Voinite, 1912–1918* (Sofia: Bŭlgarskata Kommunisticheska Partiua, 1957).

4 Members of the 13th Battalion, Royal Canadian Highlanders, 1st Division, Canadian Expeditionary Force (Liberty Memorial Museum)

Canada and Newfoundland

Canada and Newfoundland (separate from Canada until 1949) followed Great Britain into WWI as part of the British Empire. The First Division of the Canadian Expeditionary Force (CEF) arrived in France in February 1915. Most of the service of the CEF was on the western front and also in Gallipoli and Egypt.

Conscription

The militia forces of Canada and Newfoundland were voluntary, with males ages 18 to 60 serving actively and in the reserve. There was no conscription until late 1917 in Canada and the spring of 1918 in Newfoundland, and most of the recruits were still volunteers. In 1914 there were 3,110 men serving actively in the Canadian Militia. The total number of men who enlisted was 619,636.

The Army

The first CEF was reorganized from the structure of the existing militia. The Newfoundland Regiment served and deployed with the CEF. Both countries were recognized for their bravery and patriotism during the war. On the first day of the Battle of the Somme, Newfoundland's 1st Battalion lost 684 of 752 men, a casualty rate of more than 90%.[2]

The CEF was formed into 260 battalions. They were, in order of seniority (if there was more than one numbered battalion from an area it is so indicated in parentheses):

Western Ontario (2)
Eastern Ontario (2)
Toronto (10)
Central Ontario
Western Cavalry
Fort Garry House
1st British Columbia
Winnipeg (13)
Edmonton (7)
Calgary (6)
Saskatchewan (8)
Maritime Provinces
Montreal Royal Highlanders (2)
Royal Montreal Regiment
Toronto 48th Highlanders (2)
British Columbia Scottish

Nova Scotia Seaforth Highlanders
London (4)
1st Central Ontario
Kingston (3)
Quebec (7)
Montreal (8)
Montreal Victoria Rifles
Halifax (2)
New Brunswick (6)
North-West (2)
Vancouver (4)
British Columbia
Manitoba and Saskatchewan (3)
Hamilton (2)
Ottawa (2)
Nova Scotia (2)

---

[2] Philip J. Haythornwaite, *The World War One Source Book* (London: Arms and Armour, 1992), 267.

Winnipeg Cameron Highlanders (3)
Brandon (2)
Manitoba Rangers
South Saskatchewan
Victoria
Port Arthur New Ontario (2)
Prince Albert (2)
Kootenay and British Columbia (2)
New Brunswick and Prince Edward
    Island
Brockville
Victoria British Columbia Highlanders
Regina (2)
Woodstock
Montreal Highlanders
Barrie
Winnipeg Grenadiers (2)
Manitoba (4)
Toronto Queen's Own Rifles (2)
Oshawa
Nova Scotia Highlanders (4)
Hamilton MG Battalion
Victoria Fusiliers
Alberta
Elgin
Toronto Highlanders
Peterboro
Saskatchewan Highlanders
Toronto Americans
Lincoln and Welland
Essex
Winnipeg Light Infantry
North British Columbia
Prince Edward Island Highlanders
Nova Scotia Rifles
Victoria and Halburton
Perth
South Waterloo
Lethbridge Highlanders
Haldimand County Brock's Rangers
Ontario County (2)
Eastern Township
Kitchener
Saulte Sainte Marie
British Columbia Western Irish
Muskoka
Toronto Royal Grenadiers
Toronto Governor General's Bodyguard
Brantford
Peel County (2)
York Rangers (2)
Moose Jaw (2)
Wentworth County
Lanark and Renfrew (2)
Westminster
North Shore

New Brunswick
Norfolk County
Middlesex County
Durham County (2)
Northumberland
Rainy River
British Columbia Bantams
Frontenac County
Grey County (2)
Lambton County
Montreal Carabiners Mont-Royal
Central Alberta (2)
Wellington County
Cornwall Stormont, Dundas, and
    Glengarry Highlanders
Prince Edward County
Brockville, Leeds, and Grenville
Simcoe County (2)
Duke of Connaught's Own British
Columbia
Sudbury
Bruce County
Huron County
Parry Sound
Halton and Dufferin
Toronto Mississauga Rangers
Kamloops Rocky Mountain Rangers
Hamilton Highlanders
Medicine Hat
Welland County
Toronto Sportsmen
Winnipeg Manitoba Beavers
Cape Breton Highlanders
Kent County
South Alberta
Edmonton Highlanders
City of Regina
British Columbia Western Universities
Manitoba Vikings
Toronto Canadian Buffs
Toronto/Montreal Duchess of
    Connaught's Own Irish Rangers
Toronto Light Infantry
Edmonton Sportsmen
Toronto Beavers
Carleton
Toronto Canadian Irish
Moose Jaw Frontiersmen
Alberta American Legion
Winnipeg American Legion
Brant County
Toronto Bantams
Manitoba Scandinavians
Ottawa Forestry
Manitoba Men of the North
Algoma and Sudbury Men of the North

Nippising Northern Fusiliers	Montreal Forestry
Ottawa Vottiguers Canadiens Français	Montreal Kitchener's Own
New Brunswick Highlanders Maclean Kilties	Montreal Grenadiers
	Lindsay
Nova Scotia Americans	Hastings and Prince Edward Island
Forestry Battalion	Toronto Railway Construction Battalion
Railway Battalion	Montreal Railway Construction Battalion
Windsor Canadian Scottish Borderers	Siberian Expeditionary Force

The CEF also had a Cavalry Regiment, a Canadian Light Horse, and 13 mounted rifle regiments. There were two Canadian regiments that were not part of the CEF: the Royal Canadian Regiment and Princess Patricia's Own Canadian Light Infantry (see British Army).

National Archives of Canada, Ottawa
Personnel files for members of the CEF are at the National Archives in the Personnel Records Centre, along with other official records. They are indexed online by given name, surname, and regimental number (see section on the Internet).
* Ministry of Overseas Forces of Canada, service files, including those who served with British forces (**RG 150**)
* Nominal rolls (**RG 9, II-B-3**)
* Enlistment forms and attestation papers (**RG 9, II-B-8**)
* War diaries and casualty lists (**RG 9, III**)

National Archives of Canada
Personnel Records Unit
395 Wellington Street
Ottawa, ON K1A 0N3

Provincial Archives of Newfoundland and Labrador
Colonial Building
Military Road
Saint John's NF A1C 2C9

Canadian Agency of the Commonwealth War Graves Commission
Information prior to 1921 is not complete; it may be necessary to consult the War Graves Commission in Maidenhead, Berkshire, England.

Canadian Agency of the Commonwealth War Graves Commission
66 Slater Street, Suite 107
Ottawa, ON K1A 0P4

Public Record Office, Kew, Surrey, England
Canadian force courts-martial, 1915–19 (**WO 93/42–5**)

The Navy
The Canadian navy conducted coastal patrols off the coast of North America,

with 5,100 in service. More than 3,000 Canadians also served in Britain's Royal
Navy, including the Royal Naval Air Service.

Suggested Reading

Dornbusch, Charles Emil. *The Canadian Army, 1855–1955: Regimental
Histories and a Guide to the Regiments* (Cornwallville, NY: Hope Farm Press,
1959, film 1421706).

Duguid, A. Fortescue. *Official History of the Canadian Forces in the Great War,
1914–1919* (Ottawa: Ministry of Defence, 1947).

Grenville, John H. *Searching for a Soldier in the British Army or Canadian
Militia* (Fort Henry, ON: Grenville, 1976, film 1321223). Research guide to
Massey Library (The Royal Military College of Canada) and Douglas Library
(Queen's University).

Macpherson, Ken. *The Ships of Canada's Naval Forces, 1910–1993: A
Complete Pictorial History of Canadian Warships* (Saint Catharines, ON:
Vanwell Publishers, 1994). Includes a list of commanding officers by ship and
an index to ships.

Martin, Wilfred B.W. *Random Islanders on Guard* (Saint John's, NF: Creative
Publishers, 1994). Part 1 covers WWI and includes biographies of military
servicemen and women.

Morton, Desmond. *Canada and War* (Toronto: Butterworth, 1981).

Nasmith, George G. *Canada's Sons and Great Britain in the World War: A
Complete and Authentic History of the Commanding Part Played by Canada and
the British Empire in the World's Greatest War* (Toronto: John C. Winston,
1919, film 1698244).

Nicholson, Colonel G.W. *The Fighting Newfoundlanders: A History of the Royal
Newfoundland Regiment* (Ottawa: Ministry of Defence, 1964).

Riddle, David K. and Donald G. Mitchell. *The Distinguished Service Order to
the Canadian Expeditionary Force and Canadians in the Royal Naval Air
Service, Royal Flying Corps and Royal Air Force, 1915–1920* (Winnipeg, MB:
Kirkby-Marlton Press, 1991).

——— . *The Distinguished Conduct Medal to the Canadian Expeditionary Force,
1914–1920* (Winnipeg, MB: Kirkby-Marlton Press, 1991).

France

Germany declared war on France 1 August 1914. After Germany invaded Belgium and Luxembourg, the French launched their own assault against Germany into the area south of Metz, in German-held Lorraine. The Battle of Morhange-Sarrebourg proved costly: more than 300,000 French troops became casualties. The British Expeditionary Force (BEF) began landing in France in mid-August and joined the French in engaging the Germans at the battles of Mons and the Marne. These initial battles decided the eventual outcome of the war. Failing to occupy the ports on the English Channel, the Germans doomed the war to a battle of attrition. Both sides dug in along the western front, the border between France and occupied Belgium and Germany.

Conscription

In 1914 a three-year active service was required of men ages 20 to 45. Volunteers from age 18 were also accepted. The obligation was for two years' active service, 11 years in the reserve, and then assignment to the Territorial Army until age 43. Some conscription records are available at the departmental archives, but the researcher must know where the soldier was drafted or enlisted.

The Army

The pre-World War I size of the French army was 767,000 men; 680,000 were conscripts. Approximately 1.4 million men ages 27 to 36, were in the first line reserve, and another one million men, ages 37 to 43, in the second line reserve. The French army was organized into 21 numbered corps, which were formed into five armies. The corps in 1914 were:

I Lille	VIII Bourges	XV Marseilles
II Amiens	IX Tours	XVI Montpelier
III Rouen	X Rennes	XVII Toulouse
IV Le Mans	XI Nantes	XVIII Bordeaux
V Orléans	XII Limoges	XIX Algiers (Africa)
VI Châlons-su-Marne	XIII Clermont-Ferraud	XX Nancy
VII Bessançon	XIV Lyons	XXI added 1914

Each corps had two infantry divisions, one cavalry regiment, four field artillery groups, one reserve brigade, and support units.

The colonial forces consisted of volunteers from other countries: there were 12 *Tiralleur* infantry regiments from Senegal, Tonkin, and Madagascar; cavalry from Algeria (*Spahis*, Algerian Light Horse), the Congo, and Indochina (including Vietnam), and volunteers from other countries in Europe. Americans who were frustrated by U.S. neutrality in 1914 also joined the French forces, notably the *Lafayette Escadrille* (air squadron). The American Ambulance Field Service was also attached to the French army.

The famous *Legion Étrangère* (Foreign Legion) had regiments in Africa, specifically in Sid-bel-Abbés and Saïda, and a garrison in Morocco. Austrians and Germans who wished to fight on the Allied side without engaging in combat with their countries' armies in Europe would enlist in these African regiments.[3] The Foreign Legion was organized in 1831 to provide service opportunities outside of France for officers and soldiers who were not in favor with the new monarchy. In September 1914 there were four regiments:

- I and II: volunteers from France (40% French, the rest foreign nationals) who joined existing garrisons in North Africa
- III: recruits from the Paris fire brigades
- IV: the Italian Garibaldi Regiment, transferred to Italy, December 1915, after heavy losses

The first two regiments suffered such heavy losses that in November 1915 they were combined into a single *Régiment de Marche* (RMLE) and remained so until November 1918. With one exception, this was the single most decorated French regiment in the war.[4]

Service Historique de l'Armee de Terre, Vincennes

Access to French military records is restricted for 120 years from the soldier's birth, and they are available only to the veteran or next of kin. Records for the *l'Armée de l'Air* through 1918 are included with the army records. Service dossiers are in series Yb, and alphabetical classes, 1848–1914 and 1915–25, give basic information, including dossier number, which makes it easier to locate files. *Service Historique de l'Armee* records on WWI that have been opened for research:

- Etat-Major de l'Armeé (General Staff of the Army), papers, 1914–19 (**ss7–16N**)
- French military missions (**ss17N**)
- Records of the army groups (**ss18N**)
- Armies on the western front (**ss19N**)
- Armies in the east (**ss20M**)
- Army corps operational records (**ss21–6N**)
- Conscription records (**sR**)

The inventories for the N Series are published in *Inventaire Sommaire des*

---

[3]Philip J, Haythornwaite, *The World War One Source Book* (London: Arms and Armour, 1992), 177.

[4]The most decorated regiment was the Moroccan Colonial Infantry Regiment. Tony Geraghty, *March or Die: A New History of the French Foreign Legion* (New York: Facts on File, 1986), 149.

Archives de la Guerre, 1914–1918 (Vincennes: Service Historique de l'Armee, 1972–5).

Neuville, Colonel M. *Collections Historiques de Musée de l'Armée: La Grande Guerre, 1914–1918* (Paris: n.p., 1982).

Ministère des Anciens Combattants, Paris

In addition to cemeteries maintained by commissions in the U.S. and Great Britain, the War Graves Commission in France maintains memorials to those who fought and died in the service of France. In some towns there are British, French, American, Belgian, and German cemeteries maintained by the different commissions.

Records for WWI deaths for the French army are at this ministry and on microfilm at the National Archives in Paris. The information includes full name, birth and death dates, and unit and rank.

Bureau central des Archives administratives militaires à Pau

Part of the French army records are kept at the Central Archives, including pension applications from 1910 for individuals over age 60 and records of medals and decorations from WWI.

Archives Nationales Dépot des Archives d'Outre-Mer, Provence

Some records of the *Tirralleur* regiments are in the Overseas Branch of the National Archives. These documents include personnel, recruitment records, and naturalizations for:
* French West Africa (Ivory Coast, Guinea, Dahomey, Niger, Senegal, etc.), 1779–1920
* Indochina (Cambodia, Vietnam, Tonkin), 1893–1927
* Algeria, 1832–1940

Hoover Institution, Stanford University, Stanford, California
* Safe-conduct passes, French military zones, 1915–19

The Navy

The French navy consisted of mariners, ages 18 to 50, who were subject to the *inscription maritime*, a naval draft. The normal service began after age 20 for a period of five years. Volunteers were also accepted.

Service historique de la Marine, Vincennes

Naval records from 1870 are at the *Service historique*. The same restrictions apply to naval records as to those for the army. Service dossiers for WWI are in series Marine CC[7] and may contain:

* contrats de mariage, autorisations de mariage
* certificates de visite médicale
* lettres de recommendation
* parfois les compositions de l'École navale
* études rédigées par l'officier
* photographies d'identité
* dossiers de pensions

Le Maresquier, Erik. *Archives de la Marine. Guide du lecteur. Ètat de répertoires et inventaires* (Paris: The Archive, 1979).

Medical Corps

A separate medical corps existed until 1918. The *Service de Santé Militaire* has been part of the army since 1918.

Archives historiques du Service de santé militaire et musée du Val-de-Grâce

The Archives contains service records of individuals, biographical information, and history of the medical service.

*Service historique de l'Armee de
Terre*
Vieux Fort
Chateau de Vincennes
94304 Vincennes Cedex

*Bureau central des Archives
administratives militaires à Pau*
Caserne Bernadotte
64000 Pau

*Ministère des Anciens
Combattants et Victimes de Guerre*
139 rue de Bercy
75012 Paris

Service historique de la Marine
Biliothèque Historique
Château de Vincennes
94304 Vincennes

*Archives Nationales Dépot des
Archives d'Outre-Mer*
1, chemin du Moulin-de Testas
Les Fenouillères
13100 Aix-en-Provence

*Service Information et Historique
de la Legion Étrangère*
Quart Viénot
rte. Tuiliere
13400 Aubagne

*Archives historiques du Service de
santé militaire et musée du Val-de-
Grâce*
Hôpital du Val-de-Grâce
1, place Laveran
17230 Paris Cedex 05

Suggested Reading

Barbusse, Henri. *Under Fire* (New York: E.P. Dutton, 1917).

Becker, Jean-Jacques. *The Great War and the French People* (Leamington Spa, Warwickshire: Berg Publishers Ltd, 1985).

Bernard, Gildas. *Guide des Rechercherches sur l'Histoire des Families* (Paris: Archives Nationales, 1981).

Franks, Norman L. R. *Over the Front: A Complete Record of the Fighter Aces and Units of the United States and the French Air Services, 1914–1918* (London: Grub Street, 1992).

Gorce, P.M. del la. *The French Army* (London: Chatto, 1963).

Kennett, Lee. "World War I Materials in French Military Archives." *Military Affairs* 37 (April 1973): 60–2.

Morant, George de, Comte. *La Noblesse Française au Champ d'Honneur, 1914–1915–1916: Avec la Liste Alphabétique des Morts au Champ d'Honneur, Blessés, Cités à l'Ordre du Jour, Promus, nommés dans la Legion d'Honneur, la méaille mllitaire, la Croix de Guerre* (Paris: La Nobiliaire, 1916, film 1573203). French nobility in WWI, alphabetical list of dead and wounded prior to 1916.

Watt, Richard. *None Dare Call It Treason* (London: Chatto and Windus, 1964). Covers the French mutinies of 1917.

Welsch, Edwin K. *Libraries and Archives in France: A Handbook* (Pittsburgh: Council for European Studies, University of Pittsburgh, 1973).

> We are in the La Vache woods within sight of the enemy's lines. Thirty yards from them! We are on the further side of the trenches, where the terrific storm of shells rages daily. We have the honor of being the finest target that will ever be offered for a shot with a grenade.
>
> — Georges Lafond, from *Covered with Mud and Glory*

5 German sailor from the S.M.S. *Kolberg* (Liberty Memorial Museum)

Germany

In 1871, at the end of the Franco-Prussian War, Germany was unified as the Second German Empire. In 1914 Germany included the following states:

➢ *Four kingdoms*: Prussia, Bavaria, Saxony, and Württemberg
➢ *Six grand duchies*: Baden, Hesse, Mecklenburg-Schwerin, Mecklenburg-Strelitz, Oldenburg, and Saxe-Weimar-Eisenach
➢ *Five duchies*: Anhalan, Brunswick, Saxe-Altenburg, Saxe-Coburg-Gotha, and Saxe-Meiningen
➢ *Seven principalities*: Lippe, Reuß-Greiz, Reuß-Schleiz, Schaumburg-Lippe, Schwarzburg-Rudolstadt, Schwarzburg-Sonderhausen, and Waldeck
➢ *Three independent cities*: Bremen, Hamburg, and Lübeck
➢ *One imperial state*: Alsace-Lorraine

Provinces in the Kingdom of Prussia: Brandenburg, East Prussia, Hanover, Hesse-Nassau, Hohenzollern, Pomerania, Posen, Rhineland, Saxony (a territory separate from the kingdom of Saxony), Schleswig-Holstein, Silesia, West Prussia, and Westphalia

Provinces in the Kingdom of Bavaria: Franconia, Palatinate (Pfalz), Upper Palatinate, and Swabia

Conscription

In 1914 every male age 17 and older was eligible for conscription. This involved two years training in the infantry or three years' training in the cavalry or horse artillery. Following regular service, there was a four to five year period of Regular Reserve service, then five years in the "first levy" of *Landwehr* service, followed by assignment in the "second levy" until age 39; men were then assigned to the *Landsturm* service to age 45. The Empire was organized into *Bezirkskommandos* (recruiting districts, abbreviated *BKdo*), which paralleled the civil divisions of counties. Military service was raised by locality, and the troops were assigned to the local military garrison, or *Standort*.

Army

The German army was organized by regiment. The following regiments served in WWI:

Infantry	Fusiliers	
Prussian Guard, 1st–5th Foot	Prussian Guard, Jägers	East Prussia Grenadiers, 1st
Prussian Guard, 1st–5th Grenadiers	Prussian Guard, Schützen	Pomeranian Grenadiers, 1st–2nd
Prussian Guard,	Grenadiers, 1st–4th	West Prussia

Grenadiers, 1st
   Brandenburg Leiβ
Grenadiers, 2nd Pomer-
   anian, Colberg
Grenadiers, 1st–2nd
   Silesian
Grenadiers, 2nd
   Brandenburg
Grenadiers,
   Mecklenburg
Grenadiers, 1st Saxon
   Leiβ
Grenadiers, 2nd Saxon
Grenadiers, 2nd Baden
Grenadiers, 1st Würt-
   temberg
1st–8th Westphalian
   Infantry
1st–8th Pomeranian
   Infantry
1st–4th Posen Infantry
3rd–8th Brandenburg
   Infantry
1st–4th Upper Silesian
   Infantry
1st–10h Rhenish
   Infantry
1st–4th Magdeburg
   Jäger Infantry
1st–8th Thuringian
   Infantry
5st–8th East Prussian
   Infantry
1st–5th Lower Silesian
   Infantry
1st–5th Hanoverian
   Infantry
1st–2nd Hanseatic
   Infantry
East Frisian Infantry
1st–3rd Hessian Infantry
Schleswig Infantry
Holstein Infantry
1st–2nd Nassau Infantry
Oldenburg Infantry
Anhalt Infantry
1st–2nd Zoberheim
   Infantry
Metz Infantry
3rd–15th Hessian Grand-
   Ducal Infantry
2nd, 5th, 8th Württemberg
   Infantry
Old Württemberg
   Infantry

Danzig Infantry
3rd–9th West Prussian
   Infantry
1st–10th Lorraine
   Infantry
1st–4th Lower Alsace
   Infantry
Kulmer Infantry
1st–2nd Masuria Infantry
1st–2nd Ermland Infantry
Deutsch-Ordens
   Infantry
3rd–4th Silesian Infantry
Lubeck, 3rd Hanseate
   Infantry
Schleswig-Holstein
   Infantry
Hesse Hamburg
   Infantry
1st–3rd Upper Alsace
   Infantry

Fusiliers
Prussian
Pomeranian
Brandenburg
Magdeburg
Silesian
Lower Rhenish
Hohenzollern
Hanoverian
Hessian
Schleswig-Holstein
Mecklenburg
Saxon
4th Württemberg

Jäger
Prussian
Pomeranian
Brandenburg
Magdeburg
Westphalian
Rhenish
Laurenberg
Hanoverian
Hessian
1st–2nd Saxon
Mecklenburg
1st–2nd Silesian

Cavalry
1st–2nd Guard Dragoons
Lithuanian Dragoons
Rhenish Dragoons
Schleswig-Holstein
   Dragoons
1st–2nd Mecklenburg

Dragoons
1st–3rd Baden Dragoons
Hessian Guard
   Dragoons
1st–2nd Brandenburg
   Dragoons
Magdeburg Dragoons
Kurmark Dragoons
Oldenburg Dragoons
Neumark Dragoons
Westphalian Dragoons
1st–3rd Silesian
   Dragoons
2nd Hanoverian
   Dragoons
East Prussian
   Dragoons
2nd Hessian Dragoons
1st Württemberg
   Dragoons
Pomeranian Dragoons
Garde du Corps
   Cuirassiers
4th Westphalian
   Cuirassiers
Guard Cuirassiers
6th Brandenburg
   Cuirassiers
1st Silesian Cuirassiers
3rd East Prussian
   Cuirassiers
5th West Prussian
   Cuirassiers
7th Magdeburg
   Cuirassiers
8th Rhenish Cuirassiers
Saxon Heavy Garde-
   Reiter
Saxon Heavy Karbiners
Brandenburg Hussars
1st–2nd Leiβ Hussars
Brunswick Hussars
1st–2nd Silesian
   Hussars
Magdeburg Hussars
1st–2nd Rhenish Hussars
1st–2nd Westpahian
   Hussars
Thuringian Hussars
1st–2nd Hessian Hussars
Hanoverian Hussars
Schleswig-Holstein
   Hussars
1st–2nd Saxon Hussars
Guard Hussars

1st–3rd Guard Uhlans	Thuringian Uhlans	1st–13th Jäger zu
West Prussian Uhlans	1st–2nd Württemberg	Pferde (mounted)
Westphalian Uhlans	Uhlans	Bavarian Cavalry
2nd Pomeranian Uhlans	1st Pomeranian Uhlans	1st–2nd Uhlans
1st–2nd Hanoverian	East Prussian Uhlans	1st–8th Chevaulegers
Uhlans	Posen Uhlans	
1st–2nd Saxon Uhlans	Lithuanian Uhlans	
Silesian Uhlans	Altmark Uhlans	

Artillery was organized into foot artillery batteries attached to infantry divisions. The support units (cavalry scouts, engineers, medics, supply, etc.) were assigned on the divisional level.

In 1867 Prussia assimilated all the armies in Germany except Bavaria, Saxony, and Württemberg. German military records were kept at the *Heeresarchiv* in Potsdam. In April 1945 the facility was largely destroyed in bombing raids. At the end of World War II the Allied armies seized all German military records, the U.S. taking the army records and Great Britain taking the navy records (see Navy section, below). Most of the surviving original records have been returned to Germany and are at the Prussian State Archives in Berlin and Merseburg and at the *Bundesarchiv Abteilung Militärchiv* (BA-MA) in Freiburg im Breisgau.

The National Archives in Washington, DC and the Public Record Office (PRO) in Kew, Surrey still have some operational records, mostly relating to World War II. All of the records that have been returned were microfilmed. The National Archives has classified the army records in the *Collection of Foreign Documents Seized* (**RG 242**), and the PRO has classified the naval records under Admiralty class **PG**.[5] In the entire series there are more than 70,000 rolls.

The Navy

The *Kaiserliche Marine* (German Imperial Navy) in 1914 was raised from volunteers and limited conscription of mariners. The *Hochseeflotte* (High Seas Fleet) was deployed in squadrons. Capital ships over 9,000 tons that served in WWI are:

Pre-Dreadnought Battleships	Kaiser Karl der Grosse	Schwaben
Brandenburg	Kaiser Wilhelm II	Wettin
Worth	Kaiser Wilhelm der	Zahringen
Kaiser Friedrich III	Grosse	Braunschweig
Kaiser Karl Barbarossa	Wittlesbach	Elsass
	Mecklenburg	Hessen

---

[5] Apparently someone in London assigned the PG letters tongue-in-cheek to connote "pinched from the Germans." Holger H. Herwig, "Introduction to Military Archives in West Germany," *Military Affairs* 36 (December 1972):1.

Lothringen	Thüringen	Derfflinger
Preussen	Kaiser	Hindenburg
Deutschland	Friedrich der Grosse	Lützow (sunk 1916)
Hannover	Kaiserin	*Cruisers*
Pommern	König Albert	Fürst Bismarck
Schleswig-Holstein	Prinz Regent Luitpold	Prinz Adalbert
Schlesien	König	(sunk 1915)
Dreadnoughts	Grosser Kurfürst	Friedrich Karl
Westfalen	Kronpriz Wilhelm	(mined 1914)
Nassau	Markgraf	Roon
Posen	*Battle Cruisers*	Yorck (mined 1914)
Rheinland	Blücher (sunk 1915)	Scharnhorst
Heligioland	Von der Tann	(sunk 1915)
Oldenburg	Moltke	Gneisenau (sunk 1915)
Ostfriesland	Seydlitz	

The *Unterseebooten,* submarines, or U-boats, were deployed in two flotillas based at Heligoland (a small fortified island off the coast of Schleswig-Holstein). Their initial mission was to blockade the British Isles and cut them off from resupply and to eliminate British warships and sink merchantmen. The 1st Flotilla was assigned U-boats 5–18, the 2nd Flotilla was assigned U-boats 19–28. By the end of the war this had expanded to five flotillas in the High Seas Fleet, five at Flanders, two in the Mediterranean, and one at Constantinople. The UB and UC classes were added as construction of new submarines continued through the war.

German U-boat losses for WWI

1914: U5, U11, U13, U15, U18

1915: U6–U8, U12, U14, U23, U26, U27, U29, U31, U36, U37, U40, U41, UB3, UB4, UC2, UC9, UC13

1916: U10, U20, U51, U56, U68, U74, U77, UB7, UB13, UB19, UB26, UB29, UB44–UB46, UC3, UC5, UC7, UC10, UC12, UC15

1917: U28, U44, U45, U48, U49, U50, U58, U59, U66, U69, U75, U76, U81, U83, U85, U87, U88, U99, UB18, UB20, UB27, UB32, UB36, UB37, UB39, UB41, UB56, UB61, UB75, UB81, UC1, UC6, UC14, UC16, UC18, UC21, UC24, UC26, UC29, UC30, UC32, UC33, UC36, UC38, UC39, UC41–UC43, UC44, UC46, UC47, UC51, UC55, UC57, UC61, UC62, UC63, UC65, UC66, UC68, UC69, UC72, UC106

1918: U32, U34, U61, U64, U78, U84, U89, U92, U93, U95, U103, U104, U109, U110, U154, U156, UB12, UB16, UB17, UB22, UB30, UB31, UB33, UB35, UB38, UB52–UB55, UB57, UB58, UB63, UB65, UB66, UB68–UB72, UB74, UB78, UB82, UB83, UB90, UB102–UB104, UB107–UB110, UB113, UB115, UB116, UB119, UB123, UB124, UB127, UC11, UC35, UC49, UC50, UC64, UC75, UC77–UC79

The U-boats sank a total of 5,282 Allied and neutral ships between August 1914 and November 1918, grossing 12,284,757 tons. Germany lost 5,087 officers and men in the U-boats.[6]

The records of the German navy fared better than those of the German army in 1945 (see the section on the Army, above). Most of the documents seized by the Allies have been returned to Germany and are at the BA-MA under class **RM**. These documents survived because most of the records were taken to Tambach Castle in Coburg, Bavaria for safekeeping in November 1944. After the Allies confiscated these documents they became known as the "Tambach Collection." The records of the German Navy High Command, including U-boat operations, 1914–18 (T1022), are available on microfilm at the National Archives at College Park, Maryland, at the PRO at Kew, Surrey, and at the BA-MA in Freiburg im Briesgau in their original form.

National Archives at College Park, Maryland
Collection of Foreign Documents Seized [relating to WWI] (**RG 242**)
- German Foreign Ministry Archives, 1867–1920 (T149)
- German Armed Forces High Command, 1914–45 (T77)
- German Navy High Command, selected records, including U-boat operations, 1914–18 (T1022)
- Prussian mobilization records, 1866–1918 (M962)

Bundesarchiv Abteilung Militärarchiv, Freiburg im Breisgau
The original records at the BA-MA are located under the Prussian army records to 1919 (**PH**). Other army records at the BA-MA:
- Inspektion der Verkehrstruppen
- General-Inspektur des Militarwesens
- WWI diaries
- Prussian Justice Department records
- Regimental histories
- Copies of military records from other German archives
- Verlustlisten (film 0840112 ff.), casualty lists, 1914–16
- Deutsche Verlustenliste, Heer und Marine (film 0163951 ff.), casualty lists, including deaths, wounded and missing in action, sick, and POWs,1914–19
- Totenlisten Deutscher Heeresangehriger (film 0491538), list of deceased POWs, 1914–17

---

[6] V.E. Tarrant, *The U-Boat Offensive, 1914–1945* (Annapolis, MD: Naval Institute Press, 1989), 77.

Dehnen, Max. *Die Kriegsgräber in Ostpreussen von 1914/15: Die Zuordnung der auf Ostpreußischem Boden befindlichen Kriegsgräber aus den Jahren 1914/15 zu den Gefechtshandlungen* (Würzburg: Holzner-Verlag, 1966). The war graves of 1914–15 in East Prussia, now in Poland and Russia.

Geheimes Staatsarchiv Preußischer Kulturbesitz
The Prussian Archives records in Potsdam were seized in 1945. Records that have been returned are divided between two archives, in Berlin (Dahlmen) and Merseburg. Holdings include:
* Prussian government records, 1918–24
* History of Prussia and Brandenburg
* Nickel Collection of the history of Danzig
* History of Königsberg (now Kalingrad, Russia)

Generallandesarchiv Karlsruhe
* Bezirkskommando Militärangelegenheiten, 1770–1967 (film 1180367 ff.), including German XIV Army Corps records, 1870–1920, and Baden army officers' conduct registers, 1870–1920

Haupstaatarchiv Stuttgart
* German XII Army Corps records, 1871–1918
* Troop rosters for Württemberg, 1914–18
* Troop units, 1919–20
* *Dienstalters-Liste der Offiziere der Königlich Preußschen Armee: und des XIII. (Königlich Württembergischen) Armeekorps* (Berlin: Ernst Siegfried Mittler und Sohn, 1925, film 1573185). List of officers in the Prussian army: Includes the 13th Royal Army Corps of Württemberg, 1913–16.
* Württemberg Königreich Kriegsministerium. Allerhöchste Königliche Ordres, 1917–18 (film 1184960 ff.). Military decorations and indexes.
* Evangelische Kirche Neu Pasua, Slavonien. Kirchenbuch, Kriegsgefallene, 1914–18 (film 1340297). War casualties for Neu Pasua, Syrmia, Slavonia, Austria; also called Ujpazova, Szerém, Hungary; now Nova Pazova, Serbia, Yugoslavia.
* Fischer, Joachim von. *M-Bestände des Militärarchivs [1871–1922]* (Veröffentlichung der staatlichen Archivver waltung Baden-Württemberg, 1983).

Bayerisches Kriegsarchiv, Munich
* Bavarian War Ministry files, 1871–1918
* WWI Bavarian army unit records, diaries, and other documents
* Bavarian officers' conduct registers, 1850s–1918
* Bavarian soldiers' records, 1914–18
* Bavarian military court records, 1850s–1918

Gefallenen-Gedenkbuch der Stadt Nürnberg, 1914–1918 (Nürnberg: Selbstverlag des Stadtrats, 1929, film 1573161). Memorial list of war dead from Nuremberg, Bavaria: 1914–18.

Sächischishes Hauptstaatsarchiv Dresden
- Electoral Saxon and Royal Saxon army records through 1919

Niedersächsishes Hauptstaatsarchiv Hannover
- Walter, Jörg. *Personengeschichtliche Quellen in den Militaria-Beständen des Niedersächsischen Hauptstaatsarchivs in Hannover* (Göttingen: Vandenhoeck and Ruprecht, 1979, film 1917267). Inventory of military records in the archives in Hanover.
- Gefallene Söhne der Stadt Hannover, 1914–18 (film 0492813 ff.). Casualty list of Hanover soldiers, 1914–18.
- Walter, Jörg. *Personenege schichtliche Quellen in den Militaris-Beständen des Niedersächsischen Haptstaatsarchivs in Hannover* (Göttingen, 1979).

Ehrentafel des Kaiser Franz-Garde-Grenadier-Regiments Nr.2 (Oldenburg: Gerhard Stalling, 1929). Casuality list of the Kaiser Franz-Garde 2nd Grenadier Regiment, Preußen.

Niedersächsishes Staatsarchiv Bückeburg
- Schaumburg-Lippe military records, 1600s–1917

Landesarchiv Schleswig-Holstein, Schleswig
- Military records, 1867–1943, Schleswig and Holstein
- Evacuation of Heligoland, WWI

Staatsarchiv der Freien und Hansestadt Hamburg
- Veterans' clubs, 1880–1918
- German naval development, 1867–1928

Zentral Bibliothek der Bundeswehr, Düsseldorf
Holdings of the library include more than 160,000 volumes on military history, including foreign armies.

Deutsche Zentralstelle für Genealogie, Sächsisches Staatsarchiv Leipzig
The German Central Office for Genealogy is one of the largest repositories for parish registers for:
- Eastern provinces: Pomerania, Posen, East Prussia, West Prussia, and Silesia
- German parish registers for areas outside Germany: Bessarabia, Bukovina,

Estonia, Latvia, Lithuania, Transylvania, the Sudetenland, Slovenia, and South Tyrol
- Berlin, Schleswig-Holstein, Thuringia, Baden, Bavaria, Brandenburg, Hamburg, Hanover, Hesse, Mecklenburg, Rhineland, Saxony (kingdom and province), Westphalia, Anhalt, Brunswick, Hesse-Nassau, Lippe, Saarland, Schaumburg-Lippe, and Württemberg

These holdings are indexed in Wermes, Martha, et al. *Bestandsverzeichnis der Deutsche Zentralstelle für Genealogie.* 3 Vols. (Neustadt an der Aisch: Verlang Degener, 1991–4). An earlier inventory including records that were transferred from Potsdam is Langheinrich, Paul. *Verzeichnis der im Archiv für Genealogie Befindlichen Originale und Filme von Kirchenbüchern* (n.p., 1953, film 1045486). This includes records for Bessarabia, Czechoslovakia, Estonia, France, Hungary, Italy, Latvia, Lithuania, Poland, Romania, Russia, and Yugoslavia.

Military parish registers from *Garnisonkirchen* (military churches) contain records of soldiers on active duty. They may give marriages, baptisms and confirmations, and deaths. Many of these have been filmed and are cataloged in the Family History Library Catalog (FHLC) under individual parishes. The military church books of the old Federal Republic and of Berlin that are at the Center are listed in Eger, Wolfgang. *Vezeichnis der Militiä Kirchenbücher in der Bundesrepublik Deutschland, nach dem Stand vom 30.* (Newustadt an der Aisch: Archives and Libraries of the Evangelical Church, 1993). See also *Preußen Armee Findbuch der Regiments Kirchenbücher, 1714–1942* (n.p., n.d., film 0492737), inventory of military parish registers of the Prussian army.

Ministry of Defence, London
The Naval Historical Library holds all the German Official History series (through 1937) in English translation.

Bundesarchiv Abteilung Militärchiv
Wiesentalstraße 10
79115 Freiburg im Breisgau

Geheimes Staatsarchiv Preußischer Kulturbesitz
Archivstraß 12–14
14195 Berlin (Dahlmen)

Generallandesarchiv, Karlsruhe
Nördliche Hildapromenade 2
76133 Karlsruhe

Baden-Württembergisches Haupstaatarchiv Stuttgart
Konrad-Adenauer-Str. 4
70171 Stuttgart

Bayerisches Hauptstaatarchiv
Abteilung IV, Kriegsarchiv
Leonrodstr. 57
Postfach 22152
80636 Munich

Sächischishes Hauptstaatsarchiv
Archivstr. 14
01097 Dresden

Niedersächsishes
Hauptstaatsarchiv Hannover
Am Archiv 1
30169 Hannover

Niedersächsishes Staatsarchiv in
Bückeburg
Scholβ
Postfach 1350
31665 Bückeburg

Landesarchiv Schleswig-Holstein
Prinzenpalais
24837 Schleswig

Staatsarchiv der Freien und
Hansestadt Hamburg
ABC Str. 55
20354 Hamburg

Zentral bibliothek de
Bunderswehr
Uerdinger str. 50
40474 Düsseldorf

Deutsche Zentralstelle für
Genealogie
Sächsisches Staatsarchiv Leipzig
Schongauerstr. 1
04329 Leipzig

German Colonies

Germany lost all of its overseas colonies as a result of WWI. The German colonies in Africa were Togoland, the Cameroons, German East Africa, and German South West Africa. The Pacific colonies were Samoa, the Carolines, the Marianas, the Marshall Islands, and Tsingtao, China. An interesting note about German East Africa: General Paul von Lettow-Vorbeck, the commander from 1914 to 1918, was the only undefeated German commander in the war. The forces in German East Africa did not surrender until two weeks after the November 1918 armistice and were self-sufficient throughout most of the war.

Archival Guides

Täubach, Rainer. *Archive in Ostpreußen vor und nach dem Zweiten Weltkrieg unter Einschluß des Memellandes und des Soldaugebietes* (Bonn: Kulturstiftung der Deutschen Vertriebenen, 1990). Survey of archival repositories pertaining to towns in East Prussia prior to World War II, including the districts of Marienwerder (now Marynowy, Poland), Allenstein (now Olsztyn, Poland), Gumbinnen (now Gusev, Kalingrad, Russia), and Königsburg (now Kalingrad, Russia). Includes the part of East Prussia divided between Lithuania and Poland in WWI; the remainder was divided between Russia and Poland after World War II.

Welsh, Erwin K. *Archives and Libraries in New Germany* (New York: Council for European Studies, 1994).

Wünsch, Franz J. *Deutsche Archiv unde Deutsche Archivpflege in den Sudetenland* (Munich: Robert Lerche, 1958). Directory of archives in Sudetenland (including Moravia, Bohemia, Silesia, and Sudetenland), with descriptions of materials relating to Sudeten Germans.

Suggested Reading

Franks, Norman L.R. *Above the Lines: The Aces of the German Air Service, Naval Air Service, and Flanders Marine Corps, 1914–1918* (London: Grub Street, 1993).

Freudenthal, Max. *Kriegsgedenkbuch der Israelitischen Kultusgemeinde Nürnberg* (Nürnberg: I.L. Schrag, 1920, film 1609198). Commemoration of German Jewish war dead from WWI.

Gray, Edwyn A. *The Killing Time: The German U-Boats, 1914–1918* (New York: Charles Scribner's Sons, 1972).

Hazen, C.D. *Alsace-Lorraine under German Rule* (New York: Holt, Rinehart, and Winston, 1917).

Die Jüdischen Gefallenen des Deutschen Heeres, der Deutschen Marine und der Deutschen Schutztruppen, 1914–1918: Ein Gedenkbuch (Berlin: Reichsband Jüdischer Frontsoldaten, 1932, fiche 6001370). Register of Jewish casualties of WWI in the German military services, including birth and death data.

Mantey, E. V. et al. *Der Krieg zur See*. 22 Vols. (Berlin: Mittler, 1920–66). Official history of the navy in the World War.

Neumann, Georg Paul. *The German Air Force in the Great War* (London: Hodder and Stoughton, 1921).

Reichsarchiv. *Der Weltkrieg 1914 bis 1918. Kriegsrüstung und Kriegwirtschaft*. 2 Vols. (Berlin: Mittler, 1930). Official military and economic history of the World War.

Reichsarchiv. *Der Weltkrieg 1914 bis 1918.Die militärischen Operationen zu Lande*. 14 Vols. (Berlin: Mittler, 1925–44). Official history of land operations of the World War.

Reschke, Horst A. *Military Record Sources in Germany* (Salt Lake City: The Author, 1993, fiche 6001596).

Scheer, Admiral. *Germany's High Sea Fleet in the World War* (London: Cassell and Co., 1920).

Witkop, Philipp. *German Students' War Letters* (London: Methuen, 1929).

If the great conflict could have been confined to the royal families (of Europe), dear reader, we should not have cared at all.
— *Woman's Home Companion*, February 1916

6 Nishan Kerekian, Intelligence interpreter, British Mesopotamian Force, Cairo (property of Author)

Great Britain

Great Britain had guaranteed the neutrality of Belgium in the event of European hostilities. After Belgium was invaded by Germany on 4 August 1914, Great Britain declared war on Germany. The British Expeditionary Force (BEF) first embarked at French ports on 11 August.

The British Empire at War
Number served and proportion to total population[7]
United Kingdom of Great Britain and Ireland (6,200,000 / 1:7)
Dominion of Canada (640,000 / 1:11)
Commonwealth of Australia (417,000 / 1:10)
Dominion of New Zealand (220,000 / 1:5)
Indian Empire (1,400,000 / 1:225)
Colony of Newfoundland and Labrador (12,000 / 1:20)
Union of South Africa (136,000 / 1:44)

Conscription
In 1914 the British Army was made up of volunteers. The first BEF, composed of regular army and territorial forces, was virtually destroyed in the first four months of WWI. The "New Army," also called "Kitchener's Army," was formed from all volunteers and numbered more than three million men by the end of 1915.

The first conscription bill was made law on 6 January 1916. Another bill in May extended the draft to include married men. The third act on 18 April 1918 lowered the eligibility age to 17½ and raised the age to 56.

British Army
British Army records for WWI include regular soldiers, members of the Special Reserve or Territorial Force enlisted before the war, and ranks in the Royal Flying Corps prior to its consolidation in the Royal Air Force in April 1918. For records of the British Army in India please see India.

The British Army is organized by regiment. The following is a list of regiments that served in WWI ("LI" signifies Light Infantry).

---

[7] Martin Gilbert, *Atlas of the First Word War: The Complete History* (London: Oxford University Press, 1994), 130.

Infantry
Royal Scots, Lothian
Queen's Royal Surrey
Buffs, East Kent
King's Own, Royal Lancaster
Northumberland Fusiliers
Royal Warwickshire
Royal Fusiliers, City of London
King's, Liverpool
Norfolk
Lincolnshire
Devonshire
Suffolk
Somerset LI
Prince of Wales' West Yorkshire
East Yorkshire
Bedfordshire
Leicestershire
Royal Irish
Green Howards
Lancashire Fusiliers
Royal Scots Fusiliers
Cheshire
Royal Welsh Fusiliers
South Wales Borderers
King's Own Scottish Borderers
Cameronians, Scottish Rifles
Royal Inniskilling Fusiliers
Gloucestershire
Worcestershire
East Lancashire
East Surrey
Duke of Cornwall's LI
Duke of Wellington's, West Riding
Border
Royal Sussex
Hampshire
South Staffordshire
Dorsetshire
Prince of Wales' South Lancashire
Welsh
Black Watch, Royal Highlanders
Oxford and Bucks LI
Essex
Sherwood Foresters
Loyal North Lancashire
Northamptonshire
Royal Berkshire
Queen's Own Royal West Kent
King's Own Yorkshire LI
King's Shropshire LI
Middlesex
King's Own Royal Rifle Corps
Wiltshire
Manchester

North Staffordshire
York and Lancaster
Durham LI
Highland LI
Seaforth Highlanders
Gordon Highlanders
Queen's Own Cameron Highlanders
Royal Irish Rifles
Royal Irish Fusiliers
Connaught Rangers
Argyll and Sutherland Highlanders
Prince of Wales' Leinster, Royal
    Canadians
Royal Munster Fusiliers
Royal Dublin Fusiliers
Rifle Brigade
Monmouthshire
Cambridgeshire
Hertfordshire
Herefordshire
Northern Cyclists
Highland Cyclists
Kent Cyclists
Huntingdonshire Cyclists
Grenadier Guards, Foot
Scots Guards, Foot
Irish Guards, Foot
Coldstream Guards, Foot
Welsh Guards, Foot
Cavalry
Household, 1st–6th
Dragoon Guards, 1st–7th
Dragoons, 1st, 2nd, 6th
Hussars, 3rd, 4th, 7th, 8th, 10th, 11th,
    13th–15th, 18th–20th
Lancers, 5th, 9th, 12th, 16th, 21st
Line Reserve (14 regiments)
North Special Reserve
Irish Special Reserve
South Irish Special Reserve
King Edward's Horse Reserve
Yeomanry (54 regiments)
Royal Artillery Regiment
Royal Field Artillery
Royal Horse Artillery
Royal Garrison Artillery
Armoured Corps
Light Armoured Car Brigade,Middle East
Russian Armoured Car Division Tank
    Corps (formed 1917)
Support Divisions
Corps of Royal Engineers
Army Service Corps and Medical Corps

The recent publication by Simon Fowler, William Spencer, and Stuart Tamblin, entitled *Army Service Records of the First World War* (Kew, Surrey: PRO Publications, 1996), gives the most detailed description of British Army service records of the Great War.

Records at the PRO, Kew, and the Ministry of Defence (MOD), Hayes

Army service records, Burnt Documents Series, service files, 1914–20 (film 2068273 ff./ **WO 363**). This series was severely damaged during a bombing raid in 1940, and 60% of the records were destroyed. The series contains service files of the soldiers and non-commissioned officers who were discharged from the British Army from 1914 to 1920. These records are in the process of being filmed, and those that have been filmed are available at Kew, and some through the Family History Library (FHL) system. The FHL is in the process of filming surnames A–E, and the PRO is filming the other surnames. Those records still held by the MOD must be searched by that office.

Records at the PRO, Kew

Army service records, Unburnt Documents Series, 1914–20 (film 2046553 ff./ **WO 364**). These documents duplicate about 8–10% of the destroyed records, although there is some repetition with the Burnt Documents Series. Some soldiers may have enlisted as early as the 1890s. Information includes unit name and number, birthplace, age at time of enlistment, name and address of next of kin, date of discharge, and reason for discharge; may also include names of parents, spouses, and children, occupation prior to military service, and assignments in the army. Death certificates of some pensioners are included up to as late as the 1950s. Soldiers who did not claim a pension or were killed in action are unlikely to be in the Unburnt Series.

Other records at the PRO, Kew:

- Officers' service records, 1914–20 (**WO 339, WO 374**)
- Index to officers' service records, 1914–20 (**WO 338**)
- Militia records, 1759–1925 (**WO 68**). Militia known as the Special Reserve, 1908–20, including returns of officers' service, enrollment books, description books, pay lists, casualty lists, and regimental histories
- Militia attestation papers, 1860–1915 (**WO 96**), filed at recruitment, arranged by regular army regiment and thereunder by militia regiment, including discharge information
- French and Belgian certificates, deaths of British soldiers in hospitals outside the "immediate war zone," 1914–20 (**RG 35/45–69**)
- Chelsea Hospital registers, 1702–1917 (**WO 23**)
- War diaries of WWI, 1914–22 (**WO 95, WO 154**), units of the British, Dominion, and Indian armies, France, Belgium, Salonika, Egypt, and the Occupation Army, 1919—22

- Trench maps (**WO 297, WO 153**)
- British and dominion POWs in Germany, Turkey, and Switzerland, 1916 (**AIR 1/892/204/5/696–8**)
- Army POWs in Germany, July 1915 (**ADM 1/8420/124**)
- Interviews with returned POWs (**WO 161/95–101**)
- Sailing lists for Europe (**WO 25/3533–86**)
- Returning units to the U.K. or Europe (**WO 25/3696–746**)
- Regimental records of officers' services, 1764–1954 (film 0917281 ff./ **WO 76**). Regimental returns of officers' services, except for those of engineer officers, 1796–1922 (in **WO 25**). Lists different ranks held by officers, together with certain personal particulars: birth date and place, marriage, children. It is necessary to identify the correct regiment before using these records.
- Army war dead in China, 1915 (**WO 32/4996B**)
- Army Nurse Service qualifications, 1903–26 (**WO 25/39–56**)
- WWI disability pensions for army nurses (**PMG 42/1–12**)
- Service medals and awards, 1914–18 (**WO 329**)
- Orders of battle (**WO 33, WO 95/5467–93**)
- Photographs, western front (**WO 316**)
- Photographs, Gallipoli (**WO 317**)
- Photographs, Palestine (**WO 319**)
- Photographs, Salonika (**WO 153**)
- Indexes to medal entitlements, *London Gazette*, 1919 (**ZJ 1**)

Imperial War Museum, London

These records contain many diaries and journals of military personnel of all ranks, and chiefly cover the First and Second World Wars. The museum also has a large oral history collection and photographs for WWI.

Finding Aids (Cambridge: Chadwyck-Healey, 1985, fiche 6025963 ff.).

Brown, Malcolm. *The Imperial War Museum Book of the First World War* (London: The Museum, 1991).

Published Sources and Guides

The *Army List* has been published regularly since 1754 and contains lists of officers by regiment. For histories of regiments see Farmer, John S. *The Regimental Records of the British Army* (London: Grant Richards, n.d., film 0908154). For a newer guide, see Chant, Christopher. *The Handbook of British Regiments* (London: Routledge, 1988).

Regiment Nicknames and Traditions of the British Army (Aldershot: Gale and Polden, 1916).

Soldiers Died in the Great War, 1914-1919. 80 Pts. in 17 Vols. (London: HMSO, 1920-1, film 1441067). No. 81 was published separately as *Officers Died in the Great War, 1914-1919* (London: HMSO, 1919).

Holding, Norman H. *World War I Army Ancestry.* 2nd ed. (Birmingham: Federation of Family History Societies, 1991).

Holding, Norman H. *More Sources of World War I Army Ancestry.* 2nd ed. (Devon: Federation of Family History Societies, 1991).

Holding, Norman H. *The Location of British Army Records: A National Directory of World War I Sources.* 2nd ed. (Solihull: Federation of Family History Societies, 1987).

Campbell, G.L. *Royal Flying Corps: "Per Adrua ad Astra" Casualties and Honours During the War of 1914-1917* (Chippenham: Picton Publishing, 1987).

Royal Navy (RN)

The *Navy List*, published from 1814, contains seniority lists of officers from the grade of lieutenant and above. Wartime confidential editions of the *Navy Lists*, 1914-18 (**ADM 177**), are also available at Kew. Enlisted sailors are known as ratings.

The Royal Navy is organized by squadrons. The Royal Naval Division, land service, existed from July 1914 to April 1916, then became the 63rd Division of the British Army.

Capital ships over 9,000 tons that served in WWI

Pre-Dreadnought	Vengeance	Swiftsure
Battleships	Formidable (sunk 1915)	Triumph (sunk 1915)
Revenge	Implacable	King Edward (mined
Majestic (sunk 1915)	Irresistible (sunk 1915)	1916)
Caesar	London	Africa
Jupiter	Bulwark (blown up	Britannia (sunk 1918)
Prince George	1914)	Commonwealth
Hannibal	Venerable	Dominion
Illustrious	Duncan	Hibernia
Magnificent Mars	Albemarle	Hindustan
Canopus	Cornwallis (sunk 1917)	Zealandia
Albion	Exmouth	Agamemnon
Goliath	Russell (mined 1916)	Lord Nelson
Glory	Queen	*Dreadnoughts*
Ocean (sunk 1915)	Prince of Wales	Dreadnought

Bellerophen

Superb

Temeraire

Saint Vincent

Collingwood

Vanguard (blown up 1917)

Neptune

Colossus

Hercules

Orion

Conqueror

Monarch

Thunderer

King George V

Ajax

Audacious (mined 1914)

Centurion

Agincourt

Iron Duke

Benbow

Emperor of India

Marlborough

Erin

Canada

Queen Elizabeth

Barham

Malaya

Valiant

Warspite

Revenge

Ramilles

Resolution

Royal Oak

Royal Sovereign

Battle Cruisers

Invincible (sunk 1916)

Indomitable

Inflexible

Indefatigable (sunk 1916)

Australia

New Zealand

Lion

Princess Royal

Queen Mary (sunk 1916)

Tiger

Renown

Repulse

Light Battle Cruisers

Glorious

Courageous

Furious

Cruisers

Diadem

Amphitrite

Argonaut

Ariadne (torpedoed 1917)

Europa

Cressy (sunk 1914)

Aboukir (sunk 1914)

Hogue (sunk 1914)

Bacchante

Euryalus

Sutlej

Drake (sunk 1917)

Good Hope (sunk 1915)

King Alfred

Leviathan

Monmouth (sunk 1915)

Berwick

Cornwall

Cumberland

Donegal

Essex

Kent

Lancaster

Suffolk

Devonshire

Antrim

Argyll (wrecked 1915)

Carnavon

Hampshire (mined 1916)

Roxburgh

Duke of Edinburgh

Black Prince (sunk 1916)

Warrior (sunk 1916)

Achilles

Cochrane (wrecked 1918)

Natal (blown up 1915)

Minotaur

Defence (sunk 1915)

Shannon

Ships also serving were light cruiser squadrons (under 9,000 tons), destroyer flotillas, submarines, sea-plane carriers, monitors, merchant cruisers, and Q-ships (decoys for U-boats).

Records at the PRO, Kew

Naval records held at the PRO include:

- Royal Naval Air Service, register of officers' services, 1914–18 (**ADM 273**)
- Greenwich Hospital out-pensions registers, 1846–1921 (**PMG 71**)
- Charity for the Relief of Officers' Widows, 1836–1929 (**PMG 19/1–94**)
- Admiralty's Compassionate Fund, 1837–1921 (**PMG 18**), paybooks, orphans and dependents of officers killed in action or died in service
- Widows of marine officers, relatives of naval and marine officers killed on duty, pensions, 1870–1919 (**PMG 20**)
- Navy medals (**ADM 171**), including the British War Medal, Victory Medals and Stars, 1914–20, and gallantry medals
- Naval officers' casualties and ships' losses, card index, 1914–19 (**ADM**

242)
- Graves roll, all other ranks died in service, 1914–19, including names of next of kin (**ADM 242/7–10**)
- Medals awarded to foreign navy personnel
- Royal Russian navy honours and orders
- RN service book index, applications, and records
- Naval ratings' service records, armoured cars in Russia, 1915–17 (**ADM 116/1717**)
- Officers' service records, Series II, and ratings' services, 1802–1919 (**ADM 29**)
- Officers' service records, Series III, 1756–1954 (**ADM 196**)
- Royal Naval Reserve officers' service records, 1862–1960 (**ADM 240**)
- Warrant officers' service records, 1852–1922 (**ADM 196, ADM 6**)
- Registrar General of Shipping and Seamen, Royal Naval Reserve records of service, 1840–1946 (**BT 164**)
- Selected war pensions award files, WWI, 1920–72 (**PIN 26**)
- Ships' logs, 1799–1963 (**ADM 53**)
- RN Volunteer Reserve, 1903–58
- Submarine logs (**ADM 173**)
- Operational and campaign reports (**ADM 116**)
- War diaries (**ADM 137, WO 95**)

Records at the MOD, Hayes
Officers'and ratings' service records, 1891–1930, are scheduled to be transferred to Kew in 1999. Until that time direct inquiries to the MOD.

National Maritime Museum, Greenwich
Finding Aids (Cambridge: Chadwyck-Healy, 1991, fiche 6091314 ff.). Among the Museum's collections are personal papers, ships' logs, public records, published histories, and photographs. See also *Catalogue of the Library* (London: HMSO, 1968).

Rodger, N.A.M. *Naval Records for Genealogists.* 2nd ed. (London: HMSO, 1988).

Gordick, James. *The King's Ships Were at Sea: The War in the North Sea, August 1914 – February, 1915* (Annapolis, MD: Naval Institute Press, 1984).

Perret, Bryan and Anthony Lord. *The Czar's British Squadron* (London: William Kimber, 1981). Story of the Royal Naval Air Service (RNAS), which served in Russia, Asia Minor, Persia, Romania, and Austria.

Uden, Grant. *A Dictionary of British Ships and Seamen* (New York: St. Martin's Press, 1990).

Royal Marines (RM)

Marine officers are included in the *Navy List* from 1814, and RN pension records include Royal Marines. The RM divisions during WWI were Chatham, Plymouth, Portsmouth, and the Royal Marine Artillery. A special battalion of the Royal Marine Light Infantry (RMLI) was formed from each of the separate divisions. In WWI marines served aboard ships and also participated in the BEF that defended Antwerp, and some also were involved in the battles on the western front.

Records at the PRO, Kew

*   Marine officers' service records, 1837–1915 (**ADM 196**)
*   RM description books, 1750–1940 (**ADM 158**), include registers of enlistment
*   Records of service of marines who served with the Coastguard, 1900–23 (**ADM 175**)
*   RM Chatham Division, 1830–1913 (**ADM 183**), births, marriages, and deaths, wives and children
*   RM Plymouth Division, 1862–1920 (**ADM 184**), births, marriages, and deaths, wives and children
*   RM Artillery Division, 1866–1921 (**ADM 193**), births, marriages, and deaths, wives and children
*   RM Portsmouth, order books, 1806–1941 (**ADM 185**)
*   Index to RM officers' commissions, 1793–1970 (**ADM 313/110**)
*   Enlisted marines description books, including attestation registers by division and company, 1755–1940 (**ADM 158**)
*   WWI medals awarded (**ADM 171/89**)
*   WWI War Graves Roll (**ADM 242/7–10**)
*   RM 2nd General Hospital discharge records, 1918 (**MH 106/986–97**)
*   RM Eastney Church baptisms, 1866–1921 (**ADM 6/437**)
*   RM Depot, Deal, index to RM Labour Corps, 1914–19 (**ADM 313/2**)

Records at the MOD, London

Service records of Royal Marine officers commissioned after 1915, ships' muster books, and pay lists from 1878 for marines aboard ship are at the MOD in London.

RM Drafting and Record Office, Portsmouth

This office holds service records of enlisted marines after 1905 (records 1842–1905 in **ADM 159**).

Blumberg, Sir H.E. *Britain's Sea Soldiers: A Record of the Royal Marines During the War* (Devonport, Devon: Swiss, 1928).

Royal Marine Museum. *The Royal Marines: A Short Bibliography* (Southsea: The Museum, 1978).

Royal Air Force (RAF)

The RAF was not created until April 1918, from the Royal Flying Corps (RFC) and the Royal Naval Air Service (RNAS). Records of the earlier services are in the Air Historical Branch (AIR) series.

* Muster of the RAF, April 1918 (**AIR 1/819**)
* Nominal rolls, RFC and RNAS (**AIR 1**)
* Officers discharged, 1918–20 (**AIR 76**)
* WWI operational record books, RFC, RNAS, RAF (**AIR 1**)
* Casualty reports, 1916–18 (**AIR 1**)
* Recommendations for awards (**AIR 1**)
* POWs, 1916 (**AIR 1**)

Coastguard

Coastguard officers serving in Revenue Cruisers are included in the *Navy List* from 1814 onward.

Records at the PRO, Kew

* Coastguard officers' service registers, 1866–1947 (**ADM 175**)
* Coastguard ratings' service record cards, 1900–23 (**ADM 175**)
* Discharge registers, 1919 (**ADM 175/91–6**)
* Pension records, 1857–1935 (**PMG 23**)

Webb. W. *Coastguard: An Official History of HM Coastguard* (London: HMSO, 1976).

Merchant Seamen

Maritime History Archive, Memorial University of Newfoundland

Beginning in 1972 most of the records of the *Registrar General of Shipping and Seamen* that were scheduled for destruction were transferred to the Maritime History Archive in Newfoundland. The records for 1863 to 1938 and 1951 to 1976 are now at the Archive. The PRO and the Maritime Museum in Greenwich still hold samples of these registers. The Archive will respond to mail inquiries.

Guildhall Library, London

The Library holds the Lloyd's Captains' Registers, 1851–1947 (London: World Microfilms, 1988, film 1482933 ff.), which includes a card index to the manuscripts giving each master and mate under the surname of the captain. This generally includes birth date and place. See also Hall, Christopher A. *A Guide to Lloyd's Marine Collection at Guildhall Library* (London: The Library, 1985).

Uden, Grant and Richard Cooper. *A Dictionary of British Ships and Seamen* (New York: St. Martin's Press, 1980).

Talbot-Booth, E.C. *His Majesty's Merchant Navy.* 2nd ed. (London: Sampson, Low, Marston, and Co., 1943). Includes information on the Royal Naval Reserve.

Labour Corps
In 1917 the BEF raised a Chinese Labour Corps from the Shantung province of China where Japanese forces had occupied the nearby German colony of Tsingtao in 1914. Many Chinese, once in France, worked in skilled and semi-skilled jobs; others worked in building railway spurs, on burial duty, and in salvage work. Unfortunately, at the end of the war, the British delayed sending the Chinese home for an additional six months, and rioting broke out in many of the camps. All were eventually repatriated to China by the early 1920s. The official number of Chinese who served ranges between 92,000 and 96,000.[8] Other estimates place the total as high as 175,000.

There were also Labour Corps recruits raised in Africa from Egypt, the Gold Coast, Belgian Congo, East Africa, Nigeria, Uganda, and Northern Rhodesia. Except for the Egyptians, most recruits served in Africa. The Indian Labour Corps served mostly in Europe. There were also recruits from the West Indies, notably Trinidad, Barbados, and Jamaica.

Records of the Labour Corps are in the War Office records, including war diaries of the Labour Groups (**WO 95**), the Directorate of Labour (**WO 106**), report of the War Office Emigration Agency (**CO 873/578**), and the history of the Chinese Labour Corps (**WO 107/33**).

Civil Registration
Family Records Centre, London
The Office of National Statistics (ONS) and the PRO are in a new combined facility in London. The ONS holds registers of army and navy deaths, marriages abroad, and children of military personnel born abroad. Most army registers date from 1881; navy returns do not begin until 1959, and RAF returns begin in 1920.

---

[8] "Notes on Chinese Labour." *Report on the Work of Labour with the B.E.F. During the War* (**WO 107/37**).

- Regimental registers of army births and marriages, 1761–1924, index to births only
- Index to army officers' war deaths, 1914–21
- Index to army other ranks' war deaths, 1914–21
- Indexes to navy war deaths, 1914–21
- Indexes to marine registers of births and deaths, all U.K. ships, 1875–1965

Burial Records and War Memorials

The Commonwealth War Graves Commission maintains 2,500 military cemeteries in France and Flanders (Belgium). Personnel interred in these cemeteries are from the U.K. and also:

Australia	China Labour Corps	Newfoundland
British West Indies	Egypt Labour Corps	New Zealand
Canada	India	South Africa

Coombs, Rose E.B. *Before Endeavours Fade: A Guide to the Battlefields of the First World War.* 7th ed. (London: After the Battle, 1994).

Boorman, Derek. *At the Going Down of the Sun: British First World War Memorials* (York: William Sessions, 1988).

Refugees

Between 1914 and 1919 many Belgians sought refuge in England. A series of history cards (**MH 3/39–93**) gives vital information and relationships of families and individuals. Additional records are in the Aliens Entry Books (**HO 5**) and records of the War Refugees Committee, 1914–19 (**MH 8**).

Addresses

Ministry of Defence
CS (RM)2 [Army]
Bourne Avenue
Hayes, Middlesex UB3 1RF

Public Record Office
Ruskin Avenue
Kew
Richmond, Surrey TW9 4DU

Imperial War Museum
Department of Documents
Lambeth Road
London SE1 6HZ

British Library
Main Reading Room
96 Euston Road
Saint Pancras
London NW1 2DB

Ministry of Defence
CS(R)2a [Navy]
Bourne Avenue
Hayes, Middlesex UB3 1RS

National Maritime Museum
Manuscripts Section
Romney Road
Greenwich, London SE10 9NF

Commandant General,
Royal Marines
Ministry of Defence
Main Building
Whitehall
London SW1A 2HB

Royal Marines
Drafting and Record Office
HMS *Centurion*
Grange Road
Gosport, Portsmouth PO13 9XA

Maritime History Archive
Memorial University of
    Newfoundland
Saint John's
Newfoundland A1C 5S7

Guildhall Library
Aldermanbury
London EC2P 2EJ

Family Records Centre
1 Myddleton Street
London EC1 R1UW

Commonwealth War Graves
Commission
2 Marlow Road
Maidenhead, Berks SL6 7DX

Selected information for the the British Isles
Channel Islands
Civil registration for the Channel Islands is not at the PRO. The PRO does hold
Channel Island Militia records, 1759–1925 (**WO 68**).

Parks, Edwin. *Diex Aïx: God Help Us: The Guernseymen Who Marched Away,
1914–1918* (Candie Gardens, Guernsey: Guernsey Museums and Galleries,
1992). Includes a list of men, arranged alphabetically by surname, who served
in WWI.

Ireland
The Easter Rebellion of April 1916 had its roots in the sentiments of the Irish
nationalists, who were supported by the Germans. On 21 April a German
steamer carrying weapons for the rebellion was attacked by the Royal Navy and
then scuttled by her captain in the harbor of Queens-town, Ireland. A German
U-boat transporting one of the leaders of the rebellion rendezvoused with local
nationalists. Short of weapons and losing the element of surprise, the rebellion
was broken in eight days. Up until that time Irishmen had been volunteering to
serve in the BEF. From April 1916, after conscription had been introduced,
service was violently resisted by many. Ireland became exempt from conscription for the duration of the war. The strain of British military forces — some
100,000 were garrisoned in Ireland by 1919 — and level of violence were such
that Ireland was able to declare independence in 1921. The partitioned province
of mostly Protestant Ulster in the north remained under British control.

Records of Irish subjects serving abroad in the British Army are at the Office of the Registrar General in Dublin. Army births, deaths, and marriages after 1879 are indexed for 1888-1930 for births, and 1888-1931 for deaths.

The PRO also has records relating to the British Army in Ireland, 1775-1923 (**WO 35**). Records for disabled soldiers are in the in-and-out pensioners registers for Royal Kilmainham Hospital (**WO 118**).

Registrar General of Ireland
Joyce House
8-11 Lombard Street East
Dublin 2
Republic of Ireland

Kipling, Rudyard. *The Irish Guards in the Great War* (1923. Reprint. New York: Sarpedon, 1997).

Scotland
In addition to the records at the PRO, the New Register House General Registry Office (GRO) in Edinburgh holds a series of records relating to WWI.
WWI registers, 1914-18, organized as follows:
- Deaths of Scottish warrant officers
- Deaths of Scottish non-commissioned officers and men in the army
- Deaths of petty officers and men in the Royal Navy
- Army returns of births, marriages, and deaths of Scottish persons at military stations abroad, 1881-1959
- Extracts of navy returns, navy and marines, 1914-20
- Port returns, Islay, February 1918: U.S. transport ships *Tuscania* and *Otranto*
- Registrar General for Shipping and Seamen, marine register of deaths on British-registered vessels at sea, from 1855

WWI army returns of Scottish regiments, 1914-19:

Argyll and Sutherland Highlanders	Black Watch
Cameronians	Royal Scots
Cameron Highlanders	Royal Scots Fusiliers
Highland LI	Seaforth Highlanders
King's Own Scottish Borderers	Various regiments

Registrar General of Scotland
New Register House
Edinburgh, EH1 3YT

Campbell, Colin. "Scottish Regiments in the Great War, 1914-1918." *Glasgow and West Scotland Family History Society NL*, 47 (Aug 96).

Suggested Reading

British Museum. *Subject Index of Books Relating to the European War, 1914–18, Acquired by the British Museum, 1914-20* (London: Porcles, 1966).

Crutwell, C.R.M.F. *A History of the Great War, 1914-1918.* 2nd ed. (London: Clarendon Press, 1936).

Ellis, John. *Eye-Deep in Hell* (New York: Pantheon Books, 1976).

Falls, Cyril. *The Great War* (New York: Capricorn Books, 1959).

Graves, Robert. *Good-bye to All That* (Garden City, NJ: Doubleday, 1929).

Hall, H. *British Archives and the Sources for the History of the World War* (Oxford: Milford, 1925).

James, E.A. *A Record of the Battles and Engagements of the British Armies in France and Flanders, 1914–1918* (Aldershot: Gale and Polden, 1924).

Mayer, S.L. and W.J. Koenig. *The Two World Wars: A Guide to Manuscript Collections in the United Kingdom* (New York: R.R. Bowker, 1976).

Walker, R.W. *To What End Did They Die: Officers Died at Gallipoli* (Upton-upon-Severn, Worcester: The Author, 1985). Includes officers from Great Britain, Australia, and New Zealand.

Westlake, Ray. *British Regiments at Gallipoli* (London: Leo Cooper, 1996).

By now the condition of the 5th Corps was very bad. The Germans had artillery observation of all the main roads leading east and north out of Ypres and movement across the canal was becoming increasingly difficult even at night. With each day the number of casualties accumulated and wounded and gassed men lay everywhere, unable to move. There is a haunting picture of an advanced dressing station taken at this time. The operating theatre is inside; dimly, the M.O. [Medical Officer] and the two orderlies can be seen looking out the doorway. Among them can be seen the padre, a stout captain — how many men already that morning have died under his blessing, moaning some final message to their dearest in England?

— Alan Clark, from *The Donkeys*

7 Christmas postcard, France (property of Author)

8 Easter greeting card, provided by the YMCA (property of Author)

Greece

Technically neutral until June 1917, Greece failed to come to the aid of its ally, Serbia, in October 1915. Allied troops were allowed to occupy Salonika, and the Central Powers occupied parts of northern Greece. The Greek army fought with the British in Bulgaria and in the Balkan offensives. After the war, in May 1919, Greece occupied portions of eastern Turkey, and they did not withdraw until October 1922.

Conscription
Males from age 21 were liable for 18 months' active service based on a quota system, followed by ten years in the reserve. Registers of males called *Mitroon Arrenon* were kept by community, and include the date of birth, place of birth, and father's name.

The Army
The Greek army was in disarray after the abdication of King Constantine in June 1917. His son, King Alexander, allowed the army to be organized and trained by Great Britain. The army was formed into three corps, with three divisions each, a cavalry brigade, and an artillery regiment.

National Library of Greece
32 Panepistimiou
10679 Athens

Ministry of National Defense
Papagou Army Camp
15501 Holargos
Pendacon
Athens

Suggested Reading
Abbott, G.F. *Greece and the Allies, 1914–1922* (London: HMSO, 1922).

Dakin, Douglas. *The Unification of Greece, 1770–1923* (New York: St. Martin's Press, 1972).

Palmer, Alan. The *Gardeners of Salonika: The Macedonian Campaign, 1915–1918* (New York: Simon and Schuster, 1965).

9 Austrian naval personnel laying mines (U.S. Naval Historical Center)

India

India was part of the British Empire in 1914. The country contained seven Native States, 11 British Provinces, and one protectorate.

➤ *Native States*: Kashmir, Sikkim, Rajputana, Central India, Baroda, Hyderabad, and Mysore
➤ *British Provinces*: North-West Frontier Province, Punjab, Baluchistan, Ajmer-Merwara, Bombay, Madras, Central Provinces, Bihar-Orissa, United Provinces, Bengal, and Assam
➤ *Protectorate*: Nepal

The Army

Troops from British India served in Flanders, France, Gallipoli, Mesopotamia, Persia, Egypt, Aden, Sinai, Palestine, and East Africa. India provided 1.4 million troops, 850,000 of whom served outside of India. This included 55,000 in the Labour Corps, 12,000 in the Porter Corps, and 1,200 in the Syce (grooms) Company. Ranks above company commander were normally held by British officers. The Imperial Service troops were raised in the Native States. The Indian Expeditionary Force contained 130 infantry regiments, 38 cavalry regiments, 3 Royal Engineers, and 28 batteries.

The India Office List, 1886–1940: Containing an Account of the Services of the Officers in the Indian Service and Other Information. 54 Vols. (London: HMSO, 1886–1940. Cambridge: Chadwyck-Healey, 1986, fiche 6028163 ff.).

British Library, Oriental and India Office Collections, London

Records and materials on the British Army in India, Imperial Service Troops, Indian Expeditionary Force, Labour Corps, and other support troops include:
Biographical card index, civil and military employees living in India
Parish registers of baptisms, marriages, and burials from 1850
India Office Military Department

- Burial returns of officers and others in India, 1914–18 (film 2029981, L/MIL/15/22).
- Cadet papers for Indian army colleges of Quetta and Wellington, 1915–18 (film 1866993 ff., L/MIL/9/320–32). Quetta and Wellington were Indian army colleges in India. Includes name, age, date and place of birth, parents, school history, and permanent address of the cadet.
- Indian army and Indian army reserve officers' wills, 1917–21 (film 2029978, L/MIL/14/213). Wills of British officers granted temporary commissions in the Indian army.
- Alphabetical lists of casualties among British officers of the Indian Services in WWI, 1914–21 (film 2029978, L/MIL/14/128–43).

- Indian army service statements, 1914–16 (film 2029922, L/MIL/14/1–49). Includes name, rank, etc., concerning military service, as well as some pension information.
- Indian naval officers' services, 1840–1947 (film 2030094 ff., L/MIL/ 16/1–6). Gives names, birth, military qualifications, service records, dates and service periods on each ship, rank, and other confidential information.
- Military Department war book registers, 1914–23 (film 1911995, Z/L/MIL/ 6/352–7).
- Papers of cadets selected for the India Army College at Wellington, 1915 (film 1836105 ff., L/MIL/321).
- Queen's India cadetships, index, 1885–1930 (film 1866918, Z/L/MIL/9/2).
- Sandhurst cadets commissioned into the Indian army unattached list, 1902–35 (film 1886143 ff., L/MIL/9/303–19, Z/L/MIL/9/3). Includes name, age, date and place of birth, parents, school history, and permanent address of the cadet.
- Temporary British personnel enlisted or re-enlisted in the Indian army Supply and Transport Corps, 1914–19 (film 2030020, L/MIL/15/37). These men enlisted or re-enlisted for the duration of WWI. Includes name, rank, military number, British unit, and next of kin.
- Index to Indian army reserve of officers' application papers, 1917–18 (film 1886143, Z/L/MIL/9/7).
- Indian Military Widows' and Orphans' Fund, 1915–43 (L/AG/23/17/19–35).

Centre of South Asian Studies, University of Cambridge, Cambridge
University of Cambridge Centre of South Asian Studies Archives. *Finding Aids* (Cambridge: Chadwyck-Healey, 1985, fiche 6025945 ff.). Records of the British period in South Asia relating to India, Pakistan, Ceylon, Burma, Nepal, and Afghanistan. The individuals mentioned are either military or civil service personnel and their families who served in any of the above-mentioned countries.

British Library
Oriental and India Office
   Collections
197 Blackfriars Road
London SE1 8NG

Centre of South Asian Studies
University of Cambridge
Cambridge CB3 9DR

National Library of India
Belvedere
Calcutta 700027

Suggested Reading
Dodwell, H.H. *The Cambridge History of India*. Vol. 6. *1858–1918* (Dehli: S. Chand, 1932).

Golant, William. *The Long Afternoon, British India, 1601–1947* (New York: St. Martin's Press, 1975).

Mason, P.A. *Matter of Honour: An Account of the Indian Army, Its Officers and Men* (London: n.p., 1974).

Sydenham of Combe, Lord. *India and the War* (London: Hodder and Stoughton, 1915).

Seasickness had begun to affect the boys. All of them were tired of the water and aching for a glimpse of a tree. The whole sea was a mass of seething, boiling green streaked with grey hailstones as large as marbles, bouncing all over the deck, and only at intervals could any of the convoy be seen.

— from *The 469th Aero Squadron: Being an Account of Squadron Activities in the World War, 1917–1919*

10 Member of the 4th Infantry Regiment, Japanese army (Liberty Memorial Museum)

Italy

In April 1915 the Kingdom of Italy — which had previously been part of the Triple Alliance with Germany and Austria-Hungary — entered into a secret agreement with Great Britain promising that Italy would enter the war on the side of the Allies.

Conscription

Males from age 20 were liable for military service. Men categorized for Class I service performed two years' active duty, followed by six years in the reserve, four years in the mobile militia, and seven in the territorial militia. Class II service required six months' active duty, followed by seven-and-a-half years in the reserve, and then the same commitment as Class I. Class III recruits were assigned to the territorial militia for 19 years.

Enlistment was done by military district, each province having several districts. The *Uffici del Leva* (offices of conscription) records for WWI are held in the *archivi di stato* (state archives) of the various provinces. The *registro de leva* (conscription record) usually gives the *comune* (place) of birth. To identify the proper district, it is necessary to know the town of origin to narrow the search. It is helpful to use a gazetteer such as *Nuovo dizionario dei comuni e frazioni de comuni con le circonscrizioni administrative* (Rome: Società Edtrice Dizionario Voghera dei Comuni, 1966, film 0795276).

The Army

In 1914 the Italian army was formed into 12 corps:

I Turin	V Verona	IX Rome
II Alessandria	VI Bologna	X Naples
III Milan	VII Ancona	XI Bari
IV Genoa	VIII Florence	XII Palermo / Caligari

Two more corps were mobilized in 1915 when Italy entered the war. These 14 corps were organized into four armies. There were 116 infantry regiments, 30 cavalry regiments, 36 field artillery battalions, and support regiments.

Most of the *registro dei fogli* (service records) are kept at the *archivi di stato* (state archives) for each province. Italy is currently divided into 20 regions, each containing several provinces. The provinces are:

Agrigento	Asti	Biella
Alessandria	Avellino	Bologna
Ancona	Bari	Bolzano-Bozen
Aosta	Belluno	Brescia
Arezzo	Benevento	Brindisi
Ascoli Piceno	Bergamo	Cagliari

Caltanissetta	Lucca	Reggio Emilia
Campobasso	Macerata	Rieti
Caserta	Mantova	Rimini
Catania	Massa-Carrara	Rome
Catanzaro	Matera	Rovigo
Chieti	Messina	Salerno
Como	Milan	Sassari
Cosenza	Modena	Savona
Cremona	Naples	Siena
Crotone	Novara	Sondrio
Cuneo	Nuoro	Siracusa
Enna	Oristano	Taranto
Ferrara	Padua	Teramo
Florence	Palermo	Terni
Foggia	Parma	Trapani
Forli	Pavia	Trento
Frosinone	Perugia	Treviso
Genoa	Pesaro-Urbino	Trieste
Gorizia	Pescara	Turin
Grosseto	Piacenza	Udine
Imperia	Pisa	Varese
Isernia	Pistoia	Venice
L'Aquila	Pordenone	Verbano-Cusio-Ossola
La Spezia	Potenza	Vercelli
Latina	Prato	Verona
Lecce	Ragusa	Vibo Valentia
Lecco	Ravenna	Vicenza
Livorno	Reggio di Calabria	Viterbo
Lodi		

Biblioteca Militare Centrale, Rome

The holdings of the Central Military Library include materials on military affairs, Italian participation in foreign wars, the military history of the Italian states, regimental histories, periodicals, newspapers, and archival materials.

Hoover Institution, Stanford University, Stanford, California

- Italian army documents, 1915–18
- Materials relating to the Italian 44th Artillery Regiment, 1915–18

The Navy

The Italian navy's operational theater was in the Adriatic and Mediterranean seas. The commands were headquartered at Taranto and on the island of Maddalena.

Stato Maggiore Marina
Ufficio Affari Generali
Biblioteca Centrale,
Piazzale della Marina
scala A, piano III
00916 Rome

Biblioteca Dipartmentale della Marina Militaire
Viale Italia 2
19121 La Spezia

Instituto de Guerra Maritima
Biblioteca
Viale Italia 72
57128 Livorno

Biblioteca Nazionale Centrale
Vittorio Emmanuelle II
Viale Castro Pretorio 105
00185 Rome

Bilioteca d'Artglieria e Genio del
Ministero della Difesa
Via S. Marco 8
00186 Rome

War Graves Commission
Commissariato General Onorauze
di Caduti in Guerra
Ministero della Difesa
Piazza Luigi Sturzo 23
00144 Rome

Stato Maggiore Esercito
Biblioteca Militaire Centrale
Via XX
Settembre 123a
00187 Rome

Archival Guides
Bibliografia dell' Archivo centrale dello stato, 1953–1978 (Rome: Ministero peri Beni Cultrali e Ambient, 1986).

D'Angiolini, Piero. *Guida Generale degli Archivi di Stato italiani*. 3 Vols. (Rome: Ufficio Centrale per i beni Archivisti, 1981-6). Guide to the Italian State Archives.

Koenig, Duane. "Archival Research in Italy." *Military Affairs* 35 (February 1971): 11–12.

Lewanski, Rudolf J. *Guide to Italian Libraries and Archives* (New York: Council for European Studies, 1979).

Suggested Reading
Edmonds, Brigadier General Sir James E. and H.R. Davies. *Official History of the First World War, 1914–1918: Italy, 1915–1919* (London: HMSO, 1949).

Italia Marina. Stato Maggiore. Officio Storico. *The Italian Navy in the World War, 1915–1918: Facts and Figures* (Rome: Proveditorato Generale dello stato, 1927).

Mcentee, Girard L. *Italy's Part in Winning the World War* (Princeton, NJ: Princeton University Press, 1934).

Ministero della Guerra. *L'Esercito italiano nella grande Guerra* (Rome: The Ministry, 1927). Official history of the war.

Pieri, Piero. *L'Italia della prima Guerra mondiale, 1915–1918* (Turin: Einaudi, 1968).

Villari, Luigi. *The War on the Italian Front* (London: Cobden-Sanderson, 1932).

Japan

Japan declared war on Germany on 23 August 1914. By the end of 1914 it had occupied the German Pacific colonies of the Carolines, the Marianas, and Marshall Islands and the Kiachow colony in China. Japan officially acquired all of these by treaty at the end of the war. In October 1917 a Japanese cruiser was sent to Hawaiian waters as a substitute for the USS *Saratoga*, which had been transferred to the Atlantic. In 1918 Japanese forces were part of the expedition into Siberia in the campaign against the Bolsheviks. They also sent troops to aid in rescuing the Czech Legion, which had been stranded in Siberia.

Conscription

Males ages 17 to 40 were liable for two years' active service in the Imperial army, followed by seven years in the *yobi* (first reserve), seven years in the *kōbi* (second reserve), and service in the *ko kumin-hei* (territorial reserve) until age 40. Conscription of mariners was also used for the Imperial navy, and volunteers were accepted.

The Army and Navy

Most of Japan military and naval operations against Germany were conducted in 1914. Japanese forces also participated in the Siberian expedition of 1918. Most of the records held in Tokyo were destroyed in a firestorm in 1945. The following records are available to families of the deceased:

- *Kaigun shōhei rirekesho*: naval records of officers and enlisted men, 1872–1945, including name, date and place of birth, personal history, and date of death; data for enlisted men also includes births and names of male family members, previous occupation, and length of service; data for officers also includes names and dates of birth of parents, wife, and children.
- *Junkokusha meibo*, 1852–1945: honor roll of war dead

The honor roll information is at the Yasukuni Shrine. The service records are kept at the Ministry of Health and Welfare, Relief Bureau.

Official publications of other countries are useful in reconstructing Japanese history during WWI. Among them are the official history of the war in Australia by Charles Bean, volume V of the British *History of the Great War*, and the *London Times History of the War*, volumes XV–XVII.

Gaimushō, Tokyo

The Foreign Ministry has copies of the Siberian expedition files and the Tsingtao occupation in the *Meji-Taisho* (**MT**) section, 1868–1925, and is indexed in the *Gaimushō Genson Kiroku*. Some of this material is available on microfilm at the Library of Congress in Washington, DC. The Library of Congress also has

91

materials on the Japanese army in Russia located in the Albert Gleaves Papers in the Manuscript Division.

Boeur Kenshusho, Tokyo
The Military History Department of the National Institute for Defense Studies is actively studying the role of the Japanese military and naval forces in WWI. Because of the complexity of the records, the serious researcher should start here and use the extensive reference library.

National Archives at College Park, Maryland
The collection of seized foreign documents (**RG 242**) are mostly for World War II but also include some WWI documents. Records of the *Kaigunshō* (Navy Ministry), 1917–18 (NA file 8821), and the *Rikugenshō* (War Ministry), 1917–18 (NA files 14628–35 and 14399–405), contain reports of Japanese military operations in WWI. There is also material on the siege of Tsingtao in the Naval Records Collection of the Office of Naval Records (**RG 45/WA-7**).

National Institute for Defense Studies
Military History Department
Boeur Kenshusho
2-2-1 Nakameguro
Meguro-ku
Tokyo 153

National Diet Library
Kokuritsu Kokkai Toshokan
1-1-10 Nagatacho
Chiyoda-ku
Tokyo 100

Suggested Reading
Burdick, C. *The Japanese Siege of Tsingtao* (Hamden, CT: Archon Books, 1976).

Harries, Merion and Susie Harries. *Soldiers of the Sun: The Rise and Fall of the Imperial Japanese Army* (New York: Random House, 1991).

Jones, Jefferson. *The Fall of Tsingtao* (Boston: Houghton Mifflin, 1915).

Morley, James William. *The Japanese Thrust into Siberia, 1918* (New York: Columbia University Press, 1957).

Luxembourg

Invaded by German troops on 1 August 1914, the Duchy of Luxembourg was occupied for the duration of the war.

The Army

Some Luxembourgers were forced to serve in the German army. Others who were abroad when war broke out volunteered in the French army.

National Library of Luxembourg
Bibliothèque Nationale
bvd. F.D. Roosevelt 37
2450 Luxembourg

Suggested Reading

Melchers, Emile-Théodore. *Kriegsschsauplatz Luxemburg, August 1914 – Mai 1940* (Luxembourg: Sankt-Paulus Druckerei, 1977).

Trausch, Gilbert. *Le Luxembourg, Emergence d'un Etat et d'une Nation* (Anvers: Fonds Mercator, 1989).

K. Nr.
O. K. K.

Berlin, den 4. 8. 1914.

N a c h w e i s u n g

über die zur Besetzung von mobilen und immobilen Formationen be-
reiten Beamten gemäß Verfg. des B D v.2/8.14-Nr.15/14 B 2.

Lfd. Nr.	Des Beamten Dienstgrad	Name	Ist bereit zur Verwendung als Feld-Intendan- turbeamter bei mobilen Forma- tionen.	Abt.Vorstand bei stell- vertr.Inten- danturen.	Besondere Wünsche der Beamten.
1	Rechnungsrat, Geh.exp.Sekr.	Köhn	ja	ja	Als Abt.Vorstand einer stellvertr.Jn- tendantur bitte ich um Verwendung in Berlin.
2	Rechnungsrat, Geh.exp.Sekr.	Stage	ja	ja	Ich wünsche als Feld- Jntendanturbeamter bei einer mobilen Formation im Westen verwendet zu werden. Volle 10 Jahre habe ich als Soldat und Jntendanturbeamter in Elsaß-Lothringen ge- standen,während die- ser Zeit 5 selbstän- dige Manöver-Proviant- ämter geleitet,kenne Land und Leute an der Grenze und bin der französischen Sprache mächtig.
3	Geh.exped. Sekretär	Dechert	·	ja	Bin 9 Jahre bei der Jntendantur V.Armee- korps-Posen-gewesen. Bitte mich dort ver- wenden zu wollen.
4	"	Dreßler	ja	ja	Ich bitte mich ev. einer Jntendantur im Westen zu teilen zu wollen. Bin beim VII. XVI. A.K. als Beamter tätig gewesen.
5	Jntdr.Sekr.	Schütz	ja	—	Ich bitte für eine Stelle bei einer mo- bilen Formation im Westen verwendet zu werden, da ich mich französisch verstän- digen kann. Bin ge- wandter Reiter.

11 German mobilization records (National Archives **RG 242**)

The Ottoman Empire

Turkey, then known as the Ottoman Empire, signed a military alliance with Germany in August 1914. With German assistance, the Turkish army received supplies and training. The Turkish navy unsuccessfully attacked the Russian Black Sea Fleet in October 1915. During the Dardanelles Campaign, Turkish forces were able to keep the Allies from occupying the Gallipoli Peninsula.

During WWI the Turkish government instituted the policy of "Turkification," resulting in the genocide of 75% of the Armenian people in Turkey, a total of two million people. House-to-house searches of areas with Armenian populations were conducted, and the Armenians were rounded up, marched into the desert, and killed. Some of the women and children were sold into slavery, but the majority were murdered along with the men, after being raped and tortured. The genocide began in 1915, with the largest numbers of people killed in that year (there were also massacres of Armenians in Turkey between 1894 and 1896).

Conscription

In 1914 all males from age 18 were liable for two years' active service in the *Nizam*, and three years in the *Ikhtiat* (first line reserve), then 20 years in the Redif (second line reserve). Christians and Jews were banned from military service but were required to serve in labor battalions.

The Army

The Turkish army was organized into four armies, headquartered at Constantinople, Baghdad, Ezurum, and Damascus. Five more armies were added after 1914. In 1914 the army was formed into nine infantry corps, each with three divisions, increasing to a total of 70 divisions by 1918. Each division contained three regiments, a squad of cavalry, a regiment of artillery, and support units.

Ottoman Archives, Istanbul

The military headquarters records, operational records, and personnel records prior to 1918 are in the Ottoman Archives, in the Prime Ministerial Archives in Istanbul.

The Navy

The Turkish navy was commanded by German admirals, and German officers and men served with Turkish forces aboard ship. The serviceable vessels were from the German fleet, the battle cruiser *Goeben* (renamed *Sultan Yavuz Selim*) and the light cruiser *Breslau* (renamed the *Midilli*).

95

Prime Ministerial Archives,	**Museum of Military History**
Ottoman Archives	Askeri Müze
Başbakanlik Osmanti Arşivi	Komütanligi
Daire Başkanligi	Harbiye
Sirecki	Istanbul
Istanbul	

Suggested Reading

Ahmed, Amin. *Turkey in the World War* (New Haven: Yale University Press, 1930).

Helmreich, Paul C. *From Paris to Sèvres: The Partition of the Ottoman Empire at the Peace Conference of 1919–1920* (Columbus: Ohio State University Press, 1974).

James, Robert Rhodes. *Gallipoli* (London: B.T. Batsford, 1965).

Kent, Marian. *The Great Powers and the End of the Ottoman Empire* (London: Allen and Unwin, 1984).

Sachar, Howard. M. *The Emergence of the Middle East, 1914–1921* (New York: Alfred A. Knopf, 1969).

Sarafian, Aran. *The United States Official Documents on the Armenian Genocide.* 2 Vols. (Watertown, MA: The Armenian Review, 1993). The original records are part of the records of the Department of State (**RG 59**) at the National Archives.

Setin, Atilla. *Başbakanlik Arşivi Kilavuzu* (Istanbul: The Archive, 1979). Guide to the Ottoman Archives.

Toynbee, Arnold J. *Armenian Atrocities: The Murder of a Nation* (New York: Hodder and Stoughton, 1915).

Trumpener. U. *Germany and the Ottoman Empire* (Princeton: NJ: Princeton University Press, 1968).

Tugay, Emine Foat. *Three Centuries: Family Chronicles of Turkey and Egypt* (Oxford: Oxford University Press, 1963).

Weber, Frank G. *Eagles on the Crescent: Germany, Austria, and the Diplomacy of the Turkish Alliance, 1914–1918* (Ithaca, NY: Cornell University Press, 1970).

The sun is just setting and all the beach is purple, while the turrets and battlements of the castle just capture the last rays, and the Dardanelles are deep blue under Mount Ida. The sunsets here are glorious. The only thing which spoils it is the incessant bombardments of heavy guns.

— Guy Nightingale, *A Place Called Armageddon*

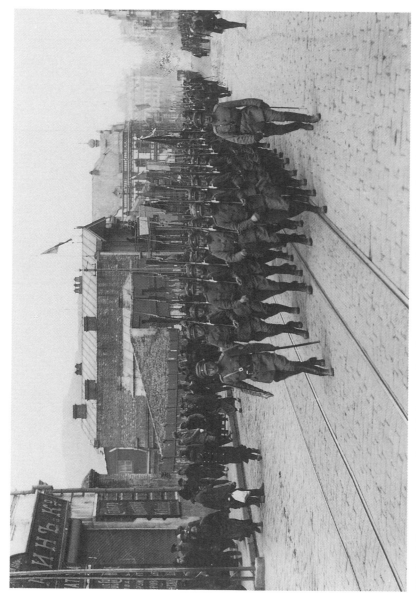

12 Czech Legion on parade at Vladivostock, Siberia May, 1919 (National Archives)

Poland

In 1914 present-day Poland existed as the Duchy of Warsaw in the Russian Empire.

Conscription

Men were liable for military service in the Russian Imperial Army (see Russia); however, service was rendered in the forces of several armies.

The Army
Russian Service

From October 1914 to February 1915 Poles served in the Russian army in the Pulaway Legion. From February 1915 to September 1917 military service was in the Russian Imperial Army, including Polish reservists in East Silesia. A Provisional Polish Government was formed in September 1917, and the Poles serving in the Russian army were regrouped into a new Polish army. This army also fought in the Russo-Polish War of 1919–20.

Austro-Hungarian Service

In August 1914 the Polish Legion was formed in Vienna as an insurrectionary force to fight in Warsaw. With the support of Austria-Hungary these Polish forces served as two brigades with the colors of the Duchy of Warsaw as part of the Imperial Army. The Legion was renamed the Polish Auxiliary Corps and disbanded in November 1916. Some Poles also served in regiments of the Imperial army, particularly in the area of Galicia.

German Service

In November 1916 the German army created the *Polnische Wermacht* with Poles from Upper Silesia and East Prussia. Attempts were made to enroll members of the Polish Legion who had served with Austria-Hungary.

The Polish Army in France

From June 1917 to April 1919 France supported the Polish army in France. Recruits were raised from Poles serving in the French army, the Russian Expeditionary Force in France, Polish POWs from the German and Austrian armies, and the U.S. and Canada. Most of the recruits were not U.S. citizens although they lived in the U.S. States represented most frequently are Connecticut, Delaware, Illinois, Indiana, Kansas, Massachusetts, Michigan, Minnesota, Missouri, Nebraska, New Hampshire, New Jersey, New York, Ohio, Pennsylvania, Rhode Island, and Wisconsin.

Polish Roman Catholic Union of America, Chicago, Illinois
- U.S. recruits for the Polish army in France, 1917–1919 (film 1993525 ff.). Includes some recruits from Ontario, Canada.

Hoover Institution, Stanford University, Stanford, California
- Recruitment records, Polish Legion in the Austrian army, 1915–16

National Library of Poland
Biblioteka Narodowa
al. Niepodleglosci 213
POB 36
00973 Warsaw 22

National Archives of Poland
Naczelna Dyrekcja Archiwów
Państwowych
skr. Poczt. 1005
ul. Dluga
00950 Warsaw

Suggested Reading

Archiwaw Polsce Informator Adresowy (Warsaw: Naczelna Dyrekcja Archiwów Państwowych, 1994). Directory of church and government archives in Poland.

Machray, Robert. *Poland, 1914–1931* (New York: E.P. Dutton, 1932).

Walt, Richard M. *Poland and its Fate, 1918–1939* (New York: Simon and Schuster, 1979).

A deposition by Captain Bertram, 8th Canadian Battalion, was carefully taken down by Lieutenant McNee. Captain Bertram was then in the Clearing Station, suffering from the effects of the gas and from a wound. From a support trench about 600 yards from the German lines he had observed the gas. He saw, first of all, a white smoke rising from the German trenches to a height of about three feet. Then, in front of the white smoke appeared a greenish cloud, which drifted along the ground to our trenches, not rising more than about seven feet from the ground when it reached our first trenches. Men in these trenches were obliged to leave, and a number of them were killed by the effects of the gas.

— *Daily Chronicle*, London, 29 April 1915

Portugal

Although the Portuguese government voted to declare war against the Central Powers in November 1914, internal turmoil delayed Portugal's entry into the war until March 1916. A Portuguese Expeditionary Force served in France and also in Africa.

Conscription
Males over the age of 21 were liable for three years' active service, followed by five years in the first levy of the reserve, then seven years in the second levy.

The Army
Two divisions of the Portuguese army served with the BEF on the western front. Some of the training was also conducted in England.

National Archives of Portugal
Arquivo Nacional da Torre do
   Tombo
Palácio de S. Bento
1200 Lisbon

National Library of Portugal
Instituto de Biblioteca Nacional e
   do Livro
Campo Grande 83
1751 Lisbon

Military Historical Archive
Arquivo Histórico Militar
Largo dos Caminitos de Ferro
1196 Lisbon

Naval Library
Biblioteca Central da Marinha
Praça do Império
1400 Lisbon

Military Museum
Museu Militar
Largo do Museu de Artilharia
1100 Lisbon

Suggested Reading
Livermore, H.V. *A New History of Portugal* (London: Cambridge University Press, 1966).

In this most serious moment I appeal to you to help me. An ignoble war has been declared to a weak country. The indignation in Russia shared fully by me is enormous. I foresee that very soon I shall be overwhelmed by the pressure brought upon me and be forced to take extreme measures which will lead to war. To try and avoid such a calamity as a European war, I beg you in the name of our old school friendship to do what you can to stop your allies from going too far. Nicky

— Tsar Nicholas II, from a telegram to Kaiser Wilhelm II

With regard to the hearty and tender friendship which binds us both from long ago with firm ties, I am exerting my utmost influence to arrive at a satisfactory understanding with you. I confidently hope you will help me in my efforts to smooth over difficulties that may still arise. Your very sincere and devoted friend and cousin, Willy

— Kaiser Wilhelm II, from a telegram to Tsar Nicholas II

Romania

Romania's sympathies lay with both the Central Powers and the Allies. Because Romania wanted to annex the Austro-Hungarian principality of Transylvania, it eventually declared war against the Central Powers on 27 August 1916. Much of Romania was occupied until a peace agreement was reached in May 1918, and after the war Romania annexed territory from Hungary, Russia, and Bulgaria.[9]

Conscription

Males from age 21 were liable for service through lottery selection. Active service was for seven years, followed by 12 years in the reserve, and then assignment to the *Gloata* (militia) until age 46.

The Army

The Romanian army was formed into four corps, headquartered in Bucharest, Craiova, Jassy, and Galatz. There was also a cavalry division based in Bucharest.

Office of the Prime Minister, Military Archives, Bucharest

Conscription records are found in the district state archives; the operational and service records for WWI are found in the Military Archives.

Biblioteca Academiei Române, Bucharest

The Romanian Academy has a large collection of memoirs and diaries from WWI.

Hoover Institution, Stanford University, Stanford, California

Among the holdings of the Institution are civilian records for Romanian Red Cross hospitals, 1916–18, and the Bessarabia *Provincil Zemstvo* records relating to the occupation and annexation by Romania, 1918.

National Archives of Romania
Arhivele Naţionale ale României
Bd. Mihail Kogălniceanu 29
70602 Bucharest

Office of the Prime Minister
Military Archives
Piaţa Victoriei 1
71201 Bucharest

---

[9] Other contemporary spellings of Romania are Rumania and Roumania.

Library of the Romanian Academy
Biblioteca Academiei Române
Calea Victoriei 125
71102 Bucharest

Archival Guides

Catalogul documentelor ţării Româneşti din arhivele statului (Bucharest: Direcţia Generală a Arhivelor Statului, 1978). Catalog of documents in the State Archives.

Stanciu, Marin. *Îndrumător în arhivele statului judeţul constanţa* (Bucharest: Direcţia Generală a Arhivelor Statului, 1977). Guide to the State Archives of the district of Constanţa.

Suggested Reading

Atanasiu, Victor. *România ín primul razoboi mondial* (Bucharest: n.p., 1979).

Fischer-Galati, Stephen A. *Rumania: A Bibliographic Guide* (Washington, DC: Library of Congress, 1963, film 0812975).

Popa, Mirecea. *Primul razoboi mondial, 1914–1918* (Bucharest: n.p., 1979).

România Ministerul Apărării Nationale, Marele Stat-Major, serviciul istoric. *România ín războiul, 1916–1919.* 4 Vols. (Bucharest: n.p., 1934–46). Official history of WWI.

Torrey, Glenn. "Indifference and Mistrust: Russian-Romanian Collaboration in the Campaign of 1916." *Journal of Military Affairs* 57 (April 1993): 279–300.

Treptow, Kurt W. *Historical Dictionary of Romania* (Lanham, MD: Scarecrow Press, 1996).

Sunday, 24th January [1916]. We are at Chortkov at last! Now that the fog has lifted, we have beautiful views of the surrounding hills. Cutting across them are dark lines in the snow, which mark the site of the trenches, and in fromt of them jagged rows of barbed wire.

— Florence Farmborough, *With the Armies of the Tsar: A Nurse at the Russian Front, 1914–1918*

The Russian Empire

One of the greatest political changes as a result of WWI was the Russian Revolution. Due to widespread unrest, need for civil reform, lack of military leadership, and critical food and supply shortages, Tsar Nicholas II abdicated his throne and ended the monarchy in March 1917. The Provisional Government issued Order Number One, which introduced committees into the regimental decision-making process, and the command structure of the military fell apart. By 1918 the Russian army was completely lacking in organizational cohesion. The ensuing civil war between the Red Army and the White armies occupied the focus of the country, resulting in proclamations of independence from Poland, the Baltic States, and Finland and the Trans-Caucasian states. An Allied force of U.K.-French-U.S. troops was sent to the aid of the Whites in North Russia in 1918–19, but they were driven out by Red forces.

Conscription
The Russian Imperial Army, headed by the Tsar, had 1.2 million troops in 1914, making it the largest standing army in Europe. Males from age 21 were liable for three-and-a-half years' service in a regiment and 14½ years in the reserve. They were then transferred to the *ratniki opolcheniia* (militia) until age 43. A separate policy was maintained for the Cossacks, who provided military service in return for land holdings. From the age of 18 men were liable for a total of 18 years' active and reserve service.

The Army
The Russian Imperial Army was mobilized from a number of peacetime corps and organized into 12 numbered armies, grouped into three fronts: western, southwestern, and northern. There were ten numbered military districts in 1914:

I Petrograd	V Odessa	VIII Caucasus
II Vilna	VI Moscow	IX Turkestan
III Warsaw	VII Kazan	X Omsk (Siberia)
IV Kiev		

Cossacks were organized into 11 armies, usually making up the corps cavalry units. Their armies originated in Don, Amur, Astrakahn, Kuban, Orenburg, Semerechensk, Siberia, Terek, Trans-Baikal, Ural, and Ussur. See also Agafonov, Oleg. *Kazachii Voiska Rossiiskoi Imperii* (Kalingrad, Russia: AOZT Epokha, 1995). History of Cossack service in the Russian Imperial Army.

The Imperial Officer Corps was multi-national. Great Russians, Little Russians

(Ukrainians), Swedes, Finns, Tartars, Germans, and other ethnic groups served together in regiments. Most of them were career military officers. Their service lists usually contain information regarding their family members, children, and hierarchy status in the nobility. In 1914 more than half the officer corps was of noble origin.[10]

The Imperial Guard units were composed of ten regiments of infantry and ten of cavalry. There were also divisions of artillery, sappers, and support.

Infantry	*Cavalry*
Preobrazhenskii	Cavalier Guards
Semenovskii	Horse Guards
Izmailovskii	Hussars
Egerskii	Cuirassiers
Litovskii	Uhlans
Grenarderskii	Horse-Jaegers
Pavlovskii	Dragoons
Finlandskii	Cossacks
Keksgolmskii	Grodenskii Hussars
Petersburgskii	Horse-Grenadiers

Rossiiskii gosudarstvennyi voenno-istoricheskii arkhiv, Moscow (RGVIA)

The RGVIA is the successor to military archives repositories dating from 1819. This is the official repository of pre-revolutionary military records of the Russian Empire. Information for officers is more complete than for enlisted men. Some of the archival collections include the documents of the General Staff (1865–1918), which was the central repository for military records for the Russian Empire, and the Leningrad Military History Archive (1934–41).[11]

Rossiiskii gosudarstvennyi voennyi arkhiv, Moscow (RGVA)

The RGVA holds extensive military records of the Russian Civil War and the wars with the foreign expeditionary forces sent to Russia after October 1917. Records run from 1917 to 1938, including the *Arkhiv Krasnoi Armii* (Archive of the Red Army), 1920–22.

---

[10] Allan K. Wildman, *The End of the Russian Imperial Army* (Princeton, NJ: Princeton University Press, 1980), 22.

[11] Patricia Kennedy Grimsted, *Archives in Russia* (Washington, DC: International Research and Exchange Board, 1993), B-4.

Voenno-istoricheskii muzei artillerii, inzhernykh voiski voisk sviazi, Saint Petersburg

The Military History Museum of the Artillery Corps, Corps of Engineers, and Signal Corps is the successor archive to the Artillery Museum (1868–1903) and the Artillery Historical Museum (1903–63). The archives hold materials relating to the artillery and military history of Russia.

Hoover Institution, Stanford University, Stanford, California

Established in 1914, the Hoover Institution collects materials on WWI including the Russian Imperial Army. Holdings include the subjects of military art and science, military drill and education, strategy and tactics, biographies, regimental and division histories, aviation, the Red Army, the Russian Civil War, and military journals and newspapers. A select list of the holdings of the Hoover Institution includes materials relating to:

Russian Imperial Army
- Miscellaneous personnel rosters and casualty reports
- Diaries and letters
- Russian Red Cross, Voon Elter Infirmary record book of patients, 1915–16
- *Kubansko-Terskii-plastanskii* Corps, 1914–17
- 2nd Uniform Cavalry Division
- 2nd and 3rd Finland Rifle Brigades at Riga, 1914–16
- His Majesty's 1st Rifle Household Troops
- 10th Corps, Sevastopol Fortress, August 1914
- 5th and 29th Infantry Divisions
- Russian Imperial air forces
- Priamur Military District, Siberia, 724th Penzen Detachment at the Khabarovsk Garrison
- Petrograd Lancers Regiment
- Zabaikal Cossack Division
- *Gvardeiskaia Pekhotnaia* Division, regimental journals
- Russian 12th Army
- Russian Imperial Army commanding officers list, 1916
- Nurse training, Petrograd, and nursing on the eastern front
- Russian Imperial Caucasian Army, 1915–16

Russian Embassy in France, 1916–24
Russian diplomatic mission in Kristiana, Norway
Russian Imperial military agencies in Copenhagen and Berlin, card file
Russian Imperial Passport Control Office, Copenhagen, card file
Russian Imperial Naval Attaché in the U.S., marriage and death certificates, 1907 and 1915
Russian Imperial Embassy in the U.S., military records, 1906–21

White Russian Volunteer Army
* Organization, 1918
* Cavalry of the White Russian Army
* Campaigns in the Civil War, Siberia, and the Crimea
* Evacuation of White Russian military and civilians, Crimea, 1920
The Turkish campaigns
Russian Expeditionary Corps in France and Persia
Association of Russian Imperial Naval Officers in America

Leadenham, Carol A. *Guide to the Collections in the Hoover Institution Archives Relating to Imperial Russia, the Russian Revolutions and Civil War, and the First Emigration* (Stanford, CA: The Institution, 1986).

Lyons, M. *The Russian Imperial Army: A Bibliography of Regimental Histories and Related Works* (Stanford, CA: Hoover Institution, 1968).

Library of Congress, Washington, DC
The Library of Congress holds one of the largest Russian collections outside of Russia. In addition to published histories and manuscripts, holdings include:
* Newspapers *Pravda* and *Izvestiia*, 1917–20
* Imperial Palace library collections of Tsar Alexander III and Tsar Nicholas II
* Photograph collection, 1910–15

For more information see Lech, Harold M. *Overview of Russian Holdings at the Library of Congress* (Washington, DC: European Division, 1997). A detailed account can be found in the *Scholars' Guide to Washington, DC for Russian, Central Eurasian, and Baltic Studies*. 3rd ed. (Washington, DC: Woodrow Wilson Center Press, 1994).

Museum of Russian Culture, San Francisco, California
Holdings of the Museum include materials relating to:
* White and Russian Imperial armies
* The Siberian Civil War
* The Caucasus Front, 1915–17
* Cossack service in WWI
* Russian Imperial troops in France
* Russian emigration to California, post-1917

Bakhmeteff Archive of Russian and Eastern European History and Culture, Columbia University, New York

Among the holdings are archival materials for:
- The Izmailovskago Regiment
- The Finlandskii Guards Regiment
- The 13th Siberian Rifle Regiment

Russia in the Twentieth Century: The Catalog of the Bakhmeteff Archive of Russian East European History and Culture (Boston: G.K. Hall, 1987).

The Navy

The Russian navy maintained a Baltic fleet based in Kronstadt, a Black Sea fleet based in Sevastopol, and a Pacific fleet based in Vladivostok.

Rossiiskii gosudarstvennyi arkhiv Voenno-Morskogo Flota, Saint Petersburg (RGAVMF)

The RGAVMF was originally founded by Peter I in 1718 and holds the records of the Imperial Russian Navy and other records up to 1940. Documents are organized in chronological groups of fonds. The collection of records runs from 1696 to 1940.
- Malevinskaia, M.E. and I. Iu. Efremova. *Spravochink po fondam Sovetskogo Voenno-Morskogo Flota*. 2 Vols. (Leningrad: TsGAVMF, 1991). Index to personal names, ships, place-names, and subjects for archival fonds.
- Mazur, Tamara Petrovna. *Rossiiskii gosudarstvennyi archiv VMF: Anntirovanny reestr opiseo [1696–1917]* (Saint Petersburg: BLITZ, 1996). Annotated register of the Russian State Naval Archives, 1696–1917.
- Malevinskaia, M.E. *Rosiiskii gosudarstvennyi archiv VMF: Spravochnik po fondam, 1917–1940* (Saint Petersburg: BLITZ, 1995). Index to holdings of the Russian State Naval Archives, 1917–40.

Tsentral' nyi voenno-morskoi muzei, Saint Petersburg (TsVMM)

The Central Naval Museum was originally established in 1709 by Peter I and holds a large collection on pre-revolutionary naval history.

Nekrosooov, George. *North of Gallipoli: The Black Sea Fleet at War, 1914–1917* (Boulder, CO: Eastern European Monographs, 1992).

Pavovich, N.B. *The Fleet in the First World War* (New Dehli: Amerind Publishing for the Smithsonian Institution, 1979).

*Russian State Military History
    Archive*
Rossiiskii gosudarstvennyi voenno-
    istoricheskii arkhiv
ul. 2-ia Baumanskaia 3
107005 Moscow

Russian State Military Archive
Rossiiskii gosudarstvennyi voennyi
    arkhiv
ul. Admirala Makarova 29
125884 Moscow

*Military History Museum of the
Artillery, Corps of Engineers, and
Signal Corps*
Voenno-istoricheskii muzei
    artillerii, inzhernykh voiski
    voisk sviazi
park Lenina 7
197046 Saint Petersburg

Russian State Archive of the Navy
Rossiiskii gosudarstvennyi arkhiv
Voenno-Morskogo Flota
ul. Millionnaia 36
191065 Saint Petersburg

Central Naval Museum
Tsentral' nyi voenno-morskoi
    muzei
Birzhevaia ploschchad' 4
199034 Saint Petersburg

Museum of Russian Culture
2450 Sutter Street
San Francisco, CA 94115

*Bakhmeteff Archive of Russian
and Eastern European History*
Columbia University
535 West 114th Street
New York, NY 10027

Dominions of the Russian Empire
Belarus
Belarus remained under Russian control when it became part of the Soviet Union, except for the portion annexed to Poland.

National Library of the Republic of Belarus
Krasnoarmeiskaya 9
220636 Minsk

Bessarabia (see also Romania)
Kern, Albert. *Heimatbuch der Bessarabiendeutschen* (Hannover: Hilfskomitee der evangelisch-lutherischen Kirche aus Bessarabien, 1976, fiche 6001388). German colonies in the former Russian province of Bessarabia, with the history of each. Bessarabia is now divided between Ukraine and Moldavia. Part was included in Romania between the First and Second World Wars. This includes a list of Bessarabian Germans who died or were missing in the First and Second World Wars.

Estonia
Estonia was occupied by the Central Powers in September 1917. Estonians served in the Russian Imperial Army until April 1917, when an Estonian army was formed.

Estonian State Archives
Maneezi 4
Talinn EE 0100

National Library of Estonia
Eesti Rahvusraamatukogu
Tõnismägi 2
Talinn EE 0100

Finland
The Grand Duchy of Finland had troops in the 13th Finnish Infantry Regiment in the Russian Imperial Army. Some also served in the 27th Jäger Battalion of the German army. In 1917 White and Red Guard units were organized. Germany helped expel the Red Guard from Finland in January 1918.

Helsinki University / National Library of Finland, Helsinki
Helsingin Yliopiston, Kirjasto
PL 15 (Unioninkatu 36)
0014 Helsingin yliopisto

Pikoff, E. *Landsmän i Ryska Marinen, 1808–1918* (Helsingfors: Frenckellska Tryckeri, 1938). Finnish compatriots in the Russian navy.

Smith, C.J. *Finland and the Russian Revolution, 1917–1922* (Athens: University of Georgia Press, 1958).

Latvia
Latvia was occupied by the Central Powers in May 1915. The Lettish Division of 50,000 troops served in the Russian Imperial Army.

Central Board of Archives
Škūnu iela II 454
Riga 1047

Latvian National Library
Latvijas Nacionâlâ Bibliotéka
Kr. Barona iela 14
Riga 1423

Mangulis, Visvaldis. *Latvia in the Wars of the Twentieth Century* (Princeton Junction, NJ: Cognition Books, 1982).

Lithuania
Occupied by the Central Powers in March 1915, Lithuanians served with Poland after WWI in the Russo-Polish War in 1919.

Lieutuvos Nacionaliné Martynas Mažvydas Biblioteka
The National Library's holdings include newspapers from WWI:
* Russian newspaper *Vestnik Evvopi*, 1802–1917 (Moscow)
* Russian newspaper *Russkaja Starina*, 1870–1917 (Saint Petersburg)
* Lithuanian newspaper *Liflandskije Gubernskije Vedomosti*, 1830–1917
* Latvian newspaper *Jelgara*, 1822–1915

Martynas Mažvydas
National Library of Lithuania
Lieutuvos Nacionaliné Martynas
Mažvydas Biblioteka
Gedmino pr. 51
Vilnius 2635

War Museum of Vytautas the
Great
K. Donelaičio 64
Kaunas 3000

Poland
See Poland.

Transcaucasia (for Armenia, see also Turkey)
At the outbreak of the Russian Revolution, Armenia, Azerbaijan, and Georgia united as Transcaucasia from August 1917 to May 1918. At that time they became three separate republics, Armenia as the Republic of Erivan. They lost their independence and became Soviet satellite republics in 1920.

National Library of Armenia
Terian st 72
375009 Yerevan

Georgian State Public Library
Ketskhoveli 5
380007 Tblisi

Manuscripts Institute
of the Academy of Sciences
Istiglaliyat st 8
370001 Baku (Azerbaijan)

State Museum of
the History of Georgia
Rustaveli 3
380007 Tblisi

Ukraine
In 1914 Ukraine was divided between the Austro-Hungarian and Russian empires. Most Ukrainians (about three million) served in the Russian Imperial Army; 250,000 also served in the Imperial army of Austria-Hungary (from the area of Ruthenia). There are military records at some of the state archives in Ukraine: the State Archives of the Ternopil Region holds draft evasion files of town magistrates, 1900–17. These files would relate to the Austro-Hungarian

army, not the Russian army.[12]

National Archive	***State History Library***
vul. Solomyanska 24	vul. Yanvarskoho Vastaniya 21
252601 Kiev	kor 24
	252601 Kiev

Subtenly, Orest. *Ukraine: A History* (Toronto: University of Toronto Press, 1988).

Wynar, Bohdan S. *Ukraine: A Bibliographic Guide to English-Language Publications* (Englewood, CO: Ukranian Academic Press, 1990).

Archival Guides

Please note that the names of some archives have changed since the breakup of the Soviet Union.

Grimsted, Patricia Kennedy, et al. *Archives in Russia: A Brief Dictionary* (Washington, DC: International Research and Exchanges Board, 1993). Please see the section in this book, "Information on the Internet," for a newer publication.

Freeze, Gregory L. and S.V. Mironenko. *Fondy gosudarstvennego archiva sossiiskoi federastii po istorii rossii XIX–nachala XX vv* (Pittsburgh: Center for East European Studies, 1994). Collection of the State Archives of the Russian Federation on the history of Russia from the late nineteenth to the beginning of the twentieth centuries.

Karasik, Theodore. *The Post-Soviet Archives: Organization, Access, and Declassification* (Santa Monica, CA: Rand, 1993).

Vinogradova, P.V. *Leningradski gosudarstvennyi oblastnye arkhivy: kratkиň spravochnik* (Leningrad: The Archive, 1966, film 1184066). Guide to holdings of the regional and city archives in the Leningrad District.

Grant, Steven A. and John H. Brown. *The Russian Empire and the Soviet Union: A Guide to Manuscripts and Archival Materials in the United States* (Boston: G.K. Hall, 1981).

---

[12] "Reports and Sources." *Russian-American Genealogical Archival Service* 1 no. 3 (January 1996): 7.

Grechkin, G. *Gosudarstvennyi arkhiv minskoi oblasti i ego filial v gorode moledechno: Putevoditel' 1917–1942* (Minsk: Arkhivnoe Upravlenie pro Sovete Ministrov BSSR, 1967, fiche 6105358). Holdings of the Minsk, Belarus Regional Archive, and affiliate archive in Molodechno.

Gosudarstvennyi arkhiv gomel'skoii mogolevskoi oblastei: Spravochink 1917–1942 (Minsk: Polymia, 1970, fiche 6105360). Holdings of the archives of the Gomel and Mogilev oblasts, Belarus.

Gosudarstvennyi arkhiv vitebskoii ego filial v polotske: Putevoditel, 1917–1941 (Minsk: Polymia, 1970, fiche 6105361). Holdings of the Vitebsk and Polotsk regional archives, Belarus.

Arkhivy Ukraïny: Organ golovnogo archivnogo upravlinnia pry radi ministriv ukraïns'koï RSR (Kiev: The Archive, 1963–75). Holdings of the national archives of Ukraine.

Derzhavni arkhiv khmel' nyts'koï oblasti: Putivnyk (L'viv, Ukraine: Vidanvnitstvo Kamenia, 1964, fiche 6105370). Holdings of the Khmel' nyts' kyy District Government Archives, Ukraine.

Gosudarstvennye arkhivy SSSR: Spravochnik. 2 Vols. (Moscow: Mysl', 1989). Descriptions of government archives of the former USSR: Armenia, Azerbaijan, Belarus, Estonia, Georgia, Kazakhstan, Kyrgyzstan, Latvia, Lithuania, Moldova, Russia, Tajikstan, Turkmenistan, Ukraine, and Uzbekistan.

Suggested Reading

Browder, R.P. and A.F. Kerensky. *The Russian Provisional Government, 1917* (Stanford, CA: Stanford University, 1961).

Cockfield, Jamie H. "Russia's Amazons: The Women's Battalion of Death in the Great War." *Command Magazine* 46 (December 1997): 80–4.

Ezergalis, Andrew. *The Russian Baltic Provinces Between the 1905/1917 Revolutions* (Cologne: Bohlau Verlag, 1982).

Golovin, Lt. General Nicholas N. *The Russian Army in the World War* (New Haven: Yale University Press, 1931).

Jones, David R. "The Imperial Russian Life Guards Grenadier Regiment, 1916–1917: The Disintegration of an Elite Unit." *Military Affairs* 33 (October 1969): 289–302.

Moore, J.R. *History of the American Expedition Fighting the Bolsheviki: Campaigning in North Russia, 1918–1919* (Hillsdale, MI: Polar Bear Publishing, 1920).

Room, Adrian. *Placenames of Russia and the Former Soviet Union* (Jefferson, NC: McFarland, 1996).

Rutherford, W. *The Russian Army in World War I* (London: Gordon and Cremonesi, 1975).

Wildman, Alan K. *The End of the Russian Imperial Army.* 2 Vols. (Princeton, NJ: Princeton University Press, 1980).

BLITZ and RAGAS

These are two of the organizations that provide research services for individuals interested in obtaining information from Russian and former USSR archives. Both services are fee-based.

The Russian-Baltic Information Center (BLITZ) in Saint Petersburg is a Russian-American company that provides genealogy services, archival research, and information services. BLITZ also publishes historical and archival reference books.

The Russian-American Genealogical Archival Service (RAGAS) is supported by the National Genealogical Society and other organizations. It determines what records still exist, their location, and makes contacts with archivists to perform genealogical searches. A newsletter is available by subscription.

RAGAS
1929 18th Street NW
Washington, DC 20009

BLITZ USA
907 Mission Avenue
San Rafael, CA 94901

Even after war was declared, the drafts arriving from the interior of Russia had not the slightest notion what the War had to do with them. Time after time I asked my men in the trenches why we were at war; the invariable senseless answer was that a certain Archduke and his wife had been murdered and that consequently the Austrians had tried to humiliate the Serbians. Practically no one knew who these Serbians were: they were equally doubtful as to what a Slav was. Why Germany should want to make war on us because of these Serbians, no one could say.

— General Aleksiei A. Brusilov, from *A Soldier's Notebook*

Полный послужной списокъ

Инженеръ Механика старш. Лейтенанта Владислава Піо-Ульскаго

Составленъ *Марта* 8 *Аня 1916* года.

I. Чинъ, имя, отчество и фамилія	Инженеръ Механикъ Старшій Лейтенантъ Владиславъ Владиславовичъ Піо-Ульскій
II. Должность по службѣ	Д. М. Афанасiй
III. Ордена и знаки отличія	Кавалеръ орденовъ Св. Станислава 3-й ст. Имѣетъ свѣтло-бронзовую медаль въ память 200 лѣтія Гангутской побѣды.
IV. Когда родился	1878 года 23 сентября.
V. Изъ какого званія происходитъ и какой губерніи уроженецъ	Сынъ потомственнаго Дворянина Могилевской губерніи.
VI. Какого вѣроисповѣданія	Католическаго
VII. Гдѣ воспитывался	Въ Морскомъ Инженерномъ училищѣ
VIII. Получаемое на службѣ содержаніе.	

13 Service sheet for Vladislav Vladisovovich Pio-Ulski, Russian navy (RGAVMF, courtesy of BLITZ)

Serbia and Montenegro

Because the assassination of the Austrian Archduke took place in Sarajevo, Austria-Hungary declared war on Serbia in July 1914. Serbia was overrun by the Central Powers, including Bulgaria, in October 1915. The Serbian army withdrew into Montenegro and Albania, bringing along many civilians. A government in exile was established on the Greek island of Corfu. In July 1917 the Declaration of Corfu was issued stating the intention to form a Slavic state. It was created on 1 December 1918 as Yugoslavia, from Serbia, Montenegro, Croatia, and Slovenia.

Montenegro was overrun by the Central Powers in January 1916. After Bulgaria fell to the Allies in September 1918, Serbian troops reentered Serbia. The population was devastated, more than a quarter of the people were dead, including more than half of the adult males. Montenegro united with Serbia on 26 November 1918.

Conscription
Serbia's army in 1914 had 29,000 troops, after mobilization the total was between 350,000 and 400,000. Males from age 21 were liable for two years' active duty in the *Narodna Vojska*, followed by nine years in the first levy of the reserve, then six years in the second levy, ending with assignment to the *Landsturm* until age 46. Montenegro had a national militia of 35,000 to 40,000 troops when mobilized.

The Army
The Serbian army had ten divisions organized into four armies:

Belgrade	Zayechar	Monastir
Kraguyevats	Ibar	Shtip
Nish	Kosovo	Vardar
Valyevoi		

There was also a cavalry division, mountain and siege artillery, and support units.

Archiv Jugoslavije, Belgrade
The records for Serbia and Montenegro are in the national archives in Belgrade, of the Federal Republic of Yugoslavia (FRY), adopted constitutionally in April 1992.

Hoover Institution, Stanford University, Stanford, California
- Serbian army soldiers' diaries and memoirs
- Materials relating to Serbian army operations in WWI

British Library, Slavonic and East European Collections, London
This collection contains historical materials on Bosnia and Herzegovina, Croatia, Slavonia, Dalmatia, Dubrovnik, Macedonia, Kosovo, Montenegro, Serbia, Slovenia, and Vojvodina. There is also a strong collection of newspapers and periodicals covering WWI.

Archives of Yugoslavia
Archiv Jugoslavije
Vase Pelagíca 33
POB 65
11000 Belgrade

National Museum
Narodni Muzej
trg Republike 1a
11000 Belgrade

State Museum of Montenegro
Državni muzej Crne Gore
Titov trg
81250 Cetinje
Crne Gore (Montenegro)

Archival Guides
Tudor-Silovic, Neva and Michael W. Hill. *Yugoslavia* (Wetherby: The British Library Board, 1990). Brief overview of library, archival, museum, and other information resources of Yugoslavia.

Milić-Grcić, Jelena. *Arhivska grada Drzavnog arhiva Srbije* (Belgrade: Graficko preduzeće "Akademija," 1960). Inventory of the National Archive of Serbia.

Suggested Reading
Corbett, E. *Red Cross in Serbia, 1915–1919: A Personal Diary of Experiences* (Banburg: Cheney, 1964).

Djordjevic, Dimitrije. *The Creation of Yugoslavia, 1914–1918* (Santa Barbara, CA: ABC-CLIO, 1980).

Gordon-Smith, Gordon. *From Serbia to Jugoslavia: Serbia's Victories, Reverses, and Final Triumph, 1914–1918* (New York: P.G. Putnam's Sons, 1920).

Petrovich, M.B. *History of Modern Serbia, 1804–1918* (London: Harcourt, Brace, Jovanovich, 1976).

Pavlovich, Paul. *The Serbians: The Story of a People* (Toronto: Serbian Heritage Books, 1983).

Stevenson, Francis Seymour. *A History of Montenegro* (New York: Arno Press and The New York Times, 1971).

> It is strange to see these enemies of ours so close up. They have faces that make one think — honest peasant faces, broad foreheads, broad noses, broad mouths, broad hands, and thick hair. They ought to be put to threshing, reaping, and apple picking. They look just as kindly as our own peasants in Friesland.
>
> — Erich Maria Remarque, from *All Quiet on the Western Front*

14 U.S. Navy seamen from the U.S.S. *Buffalo* (property of Author)

South Africa

As part of the British Empire, South Africa followed Great Britain into the war. Troops from South Africa served in Egypt and then transferred to France, where they served on the western front. South Africans also served with British forces against the German colonies in Africa. Whites from South Africa forbade blacks by law from bearing arms; blacks served only in support units.

Conscription

Service in the regular army was volunteer. Males between ages 16 and 25 were registered in a draft lottery for reserve service in the Active Citizen Force (ACF).

The Army

The Union Defence Force was formed in 1912. The South African army consisted of five mounted rifle regiments. There were also two rifle regiments in the British Army. The ACF contained 12 mounted rifle regiments.

South African National Defence Force (SANDF), Pretoria

Military personnel files dating from 1912 are held at the SANDF in the Documentation Service.

Natal State Archives, Pietermaritzburg

Hershensohnn collection, 1899–1918 (film 1295386 ff.). Includes list of South African war dead from WWI, organized by company, with surname, initials, rank, and abbreviations for place, cause, and date of death.

Cape State Archives, Cape Town

This archive holds military parish records, 1806–1921.

South African National Defence
Force
The Director
Documentation Service
Private Bag X289
Pretoria 0001

Natal State Archives
Pietermaritzburg

Cape State Archives
Private Bag 9025
Cape Town

Suggested Reading

Adler, F.B. *The History of the Transvaal Horse Artillery* (Johannesburg: n.p., 1927).

—— . *The South African Field Artillery in German East Africa and Palestine, 1915–1919* (Pretoria: South African National War Museum, 1958). Information includes roll of honor, honors and awards, and lists of officers, warrant officers, and non-commissioned officers in the South African Field Artillery (SAFA).

Buchan, J. *The History of the South African Forces in France* (London: Nelson, 1920).

Davenport, T.R.H. *South Africa: A Modern History* (Toronto: University of Toronto Press, 1987).

Directory of Manuscript Collections in Southern Africa: 1985 (Cape Town: South African Library, 1986).

Farwell, Byron. *The Great War in Africa* (New York: W. W. Norton, 1986).

Green, M.S. *The Making of the Union of South Africa* (London: Longmans, Green, 1947).

South Africa Government Archives. *List of Finding Aids in Archives Depots* (Pretoria: Government Archives, 1969, film 0990176). Inventories of collections of the Cape Archives Depot, Natal Archives Depot, Free State Archives Depot, Transvaal Archives Depot, Central Archives Depot, and Archives Depot of the South-West Africa Territory (now called Namibia).

The Union of South Africa and the Great War, 1914–1918 (Pretoria: Government Printers' Stationery Office, 1924).

At the Battle of Belleau Wood:

When the order for the advance came the sergeant [Gunnery Sergeant Dan Daly, double recipient of the Medal of Honor] ran out to the center of his platoon; he swung his bayoneted rifle over his head with a forward sweep. He said to the men of his platoon "Come on, you sons of bitches. Do you want to live forever?" That did it. With a yell, the Marines came up from the ground and stormed across the bulletswept field— to Hell.

— Floyd Gibbons, from *And They Thought We Wouldn't Fight*

The United States

For the first three years of the war the U.S. maintained an isolationist position, but U-boat activity off the North American coast eventually drew the country into the conflict. War was declared on Germany 6 April 1917. The first troops were sent to Europe in late June.

Before the official declaration of war, some U.S. citizens volunteered to serve in British and French forces, notably the *Lafayette Escadrille*, a squadron in France's *Aviation Militaire,* and also the Foreign Legion. The American Ambulance Field Service was organized in 1914 and served on the western front in France and Belgium and in Serbia later in the war. The American Red Cross sent nurses to France to work along the Allied lines on the western front.

Some Americans were recruited for what was known as the American Legion in the Canadian Expeditionary Force (CEF). More than 20% deserted in training. They deployed as the 97th Overseas Battalion of the CEF in September 1916. After arriving in England the Legion was divided into other regiments, causing many resignations, as the volunteers were led to believe they would be allowed to fight as local units.

Conscription

The first national conscription act in the U.S. was enacted during the Civil War, but it was widely denounced as un-American. By the outbreak of WWI, the national draft was considered an acceptable method of raising an army.[13] In 1914 the U.S. had a regular army of 127,588 and a National Guard of 181,620. On 18 May 1917 the Selective Service Act was passed, authorizing the temporary increase in the military establishment of the U.S.

The Selective Service System (**RG 163**) was responsible for the process of selecting men for induction into military service, from the initial registration to the actual delivery of men to military training camps. Local boards were established for each county or similar subdivision in each state and for each city or county with a population greater than 30,000. The boards were charged with the registration, determination of order and serial numbers, classification, call, and entrainment of draftees. By the end of 1917 the army had half a million draftees and 233,000 volunteers.

---

[13] Please note that conscription did not apply to the navy or the Marine Corps in the U.S.; these were all-volunteer services.

During WWI there were three registrations:

➤ *5 June 1917*: all men between ages 21 and 31
➤ *5 June 1918*: men who had reached age 21 after 5 June 1917; supplemental registration 24 August 1918 for those reaching age 21 after 5 June 1918
➤ *12 September 1918*: men ages 18 through 45

There are 24 million cards of men who registered for the draft, about 23% of the population in 1918. General information shown includes order and serial number (assigned by the Selective Service System), full name, date and place of birth, race, citizenship, occupation, personal description, and signature. The cards are organized alphabetically by county, except for Connecticut, Massachusetts, and Rhode Island, where they are organized alphabetically statewide.

Service numbers were first assigned to enlisted personnel in the army, navy, marines, and Coast Guard on 28 February 1918. Headquarters and recruiting offices were given random batches of numbers. Officers were not assigned service numbers until 1921.

Not all of the men who registered for the draft actually served in the military, and not all of the men who served in the military registered for the draft. These registration cards are not military service records and contain no information about an individual's military service. In rural areas a registrant's card can be found by knowing his name and the county in which he registered. For larger cities or counties, there may be many draft boards within the same geographic area. Researchers may need to consult a 1917 city directory to determine the address of an individual from the following cities or counties:

Albany, New York	Milwaukee, Wisconsin
Atlanta, Georgia	Minneapolis, Minnesota
Baltimore, Maryland	Newark, New Jersey
Boston, Massachusetts	New Orleans, Louisiana
Buffalo, New York	New York City, New York
Chicago, Illinois	Philadelphia, Pennsylvania
Cincinnati, Ohio	Pittsburgh, Pennsylvania
Cleveland, Ohio	Providence, Rhode Island
Indianapolis, Indiana	Saint Louis, Missouri
Jersey City, New Jersey	Saint Paul, Minnesota
Kansas City, Missouri	San Francisco, California
Los Angeles, California	Seattle, Washington
Louisville, Kentucky	Syracuse, New York
Luzerne County, Pennsylvania	Washington, DC

There is also a set of Selective Service System draft board maps (film 1498803), some showing boundaries of the draft board, others just street and road maps. The maps were filmed in the order as follows:

Birmingham, Alabama
Los Angeles, California
San Diego, California
Denver, Colorado
Bridgeport, Connecticut
Hartford, Connecticut
New Haven, Connecticut
District of Columbia
Atlanta, Georgia
Chicago, Illinois
Indianapolis, Indiana
Louisville, Kentucky
New Orleans, Louisiana
Baltimore, Maryland
Boston, Massachusetts
Minneapolis, Minnesota
Saint Paul, Minnesota
Kansas City, Missouri
Jersey City, New Jersey
Albany County, New York
Rensselaer County, New York
Bronx, New York

Brooklyn, New York
Manhattan, New York
Queens, New York
Richmond, New York
Staten Island, New York
Rochester, New York
Schenectady, New York
Syracuse, New York
Buffalo, New York
Cincinnati, Ohio
Cleveland, Ohio
Toledo, Ohio
Allegheny County, Pennsylvania
Luzerne County, Pennsylvania
Pittsburgh, Pennsylvania
Philadelphia, Pennsylvania
Reading, Pennsylvania
Westmoreland, Pennsylvania
Dallas, Texas
Seattle, Washington
Milwaukee, Wisconsin

The draft registration cards are at the National Archives in East Point, Georgia, on film, and some in duplicate at state archives, historical societies, and state adjutant general or Department of Veterans' Affairs offices. They are listed below by state and district, followed by Puerto Rico. The last reel in each series contains registrations for "Indians, insane, prisoners, and late registration." The other Selective Service (**RG 163**) records—docket books, inductions, delinquents and deserters, and district boards—are at the regional branches of the National Archives, and copies are at some state facilities. They are arranged as follows:

Region	Records held for these states
New England: Waltham (MA)	Connecticut, Maine, Massachusetts, New Hampshire, Rhode Island, Vermont
Northeast: New York (NY)	New Jersey, New York, Puerto Rico
Mid Atlantic: Philadelphia (PA)	Delaware, District of Columbia, Maryland, Pennsylvania, Virginia
Southeast: East Point (GA)	All of the U.S. (registrations only); Alabama, Florida, Georgia, Kentucky, Mississippi, North Carolina, South Carolina, Tennessee

Region	Records held for these states
Great Lakes: Chicago (IL)	Illinois, Indiana, Michigan, Minnesota, Ohio, Wisconsin
Central Plains: Kansas City (MO)	Iowa, Kansas, Missouri, Nebraska
Southwest: Fort Worth (TX)	Arkansas, Louisiana, Oklahoma, Texas
Rocky Mountain: Denver (CO)	Colorado, Montana, New Mexico, North Dakota, South Dakota, Utah, Wyoming
Pacific Southwest: Laguna Niguel (CA)	Arizona, California (district boards); Arizona, southern California, Clark County, Nevada (docket books)
Pacific Northwest: Seattle (WA)	Idaho, Oregon, Washington
Pacific Sierra: San Bruno (CA)	California, Hawaii, Nevada (deserters' records); Hawaii, Nevada (except for Clark County), northern California (docket books)
Alaska: Anchorage	Alaska
Washington, DC	Panama, Canada, Cuba, Dominican Republic, France, Switzerland, United Kingdom (declarations of intention to become U.S. citizens); aliens residing in the U.S.; Canadian and British Expeditionary Forces residing in the U.S.

The Army

The National Guard units headquartered in the states had been recently mobilized for service in the Punitive Expedition to Mexico in 1916. This experience gave the U.S. Army a head start on training, which considerably shortened the training and mobilization time required in 1917. As of 1918, 2,149,000 draftees and 198,000 volunteers had served in the U.S. Army in WWI. Existing records for officers separated after 1917 and enlisted personnel discharged after 1912 are kept at the National Personnel Records Center (NPRC) in Saint Louis, Missouri. A fire at the NPRC in 1973 destroyed many compiled service folders of enlisted men, 1912–56, and officers, 1917–56. Morning reports, 1917–74, are also held at the NPRC.

Nine Base Sections (**RG 120**) were established in Europe as centers for movement of supplies and troops for the American Expeditionary Force (AEF). The section headquarters were as follows:

Base Section 1	London	**Base Section 7**
Saint-Nazaire	**Base Section 4**	La Pallice
Nantes	Le Havre (11/17)	La Rochelle
Base Section 2	**Base Section 5**	**Base Section 8**
Bordeaux	Brest	Padua (Italy)
Base Section 3	**Base Section 6**	**Base Section 9**
Le Havre (8/17)	Marseille	Antwerp (Belgium)

National Archives, Washington, DC

Records of the U.S. Army and Americans serving in WWI include:

Records of the AEF (**RG 120**)

- 27th Division (formerly New York National Guard), 1917–19 (M819)
- Historical Section, including war diaries, Native Americans in the AEF, unit histories, military observers with the French army, etc.
- Chief of Air Service: casualty card file, 1917–19, records of Balloon Wing companies, etc. (M990)
- General Staff: Prisoner of War Division, POW labor companies, etc.
- Chief Surgeon: daily and monthly casualty reports, 1917–19, records of hospitals and hospital units, Red Cross hospitals, infantry division medical officers' records, etc.
- Records of the District of Paris
- Records of the First–Third armies
- Records of I–IX Corps
- American forces in France, 1919–20
- American forces in Germany, 1918–23
- American Polish Relief Expedition, 1919–21
- AEF, North Russia, 1917–19 (M924)
- Cartographic records, including Belgian, British, French, Italian, Austro-Hungarian, German, and Siberian maps. For more information, see Burch, Franklin W. *Preliminary Inventory of the Cartographic Records of the American Expeditionary Forces, 1917–21*. PI 165 (Washington, DC, 1966).
- Still pictures, 1915–20

Army Air Forces (**RG 18**)

- Air Service and Air Corps units, 1917–41
- Records of air fields, 1917–41

Records of U.S. Army Mobile Units (**RG 391**)

- Field artillery regiments, coast artillery units, mine planters
- 1st–15th Cavalry regiments
- Corps of Engineers battalion and company records, muster rolls, field returns, etc.
- Infantry divisions and brigades

- WWI units: fire truck and hose companies, guard and fire companies, mobile laundry companies, medical supply units, motor commands, motor repair units, motor transport companies, motor truck companies, ordnance depot companies, reserve service battalions, salvage companies, signal service companies, and guard battalions

Records of U.S. Army Coast Artillery Districts and Defenses (**RG 392**)
- Coast artillery districts
- Coast and harbor defenses

Records of the U.S. Army Continental Commands (**RG 393**). The continental U.S. was divided into six geographical (or territorial) departments from 1917–20: Central, East, Northeast, Southeast, Southern, and Western.

Records of the U.S. Army Overseas Operations and Commands (**RG 395**)
- AEF, Siberia, 1918–20 (M917)
- Punitive Expedition to Mexico, 1916–7
- Army troops in China, 1912–38
- Puerto Rican Provisional Regiment of Infantry, 1918–19

Records of the Adjutant General's Office (**RG 407**)
- Cross index to central files, 1917–39 (T822)

Records of the Office of the Judge Advocate General (**RG 153**)
- Ledgers of courts-martial convictions in the AEF, 1917–19

The U.S. Army History Institute, Carlisle Barracks, Pennsylvania

A survey was taken in 1975 of WWI veterans on selected subjects, such as boot camp, the war in France, field artillery, the AEF in North Russia and Siberia, troop ships, etc. The survey is available on microfilm at the Institute. The Institute also holds the U.S. Army WWI Signal Corps photo collection and more than 10,000 volumes and monographs on WWI. For more information see *World War I Manuscripts: The World War I Survey*. Special Bibliography No. 20 (Carlisle, PA: The Institute, 1986). Contents of their WWI collection listed in a composite bibliography are:

- Mobilization and manpower
- Personnel management
- Training
- Overseas deployment
- Strategy/tactics
- Casualties
- Battles/operations
- Units (divisions through 1919)
- Air aspects/service
- Artillery
- Medical
- Transportation

- Other arms/services/functions
- Logistics
- Weapons/equipment
- Uniforms/insignia
- Miscellaneous
- Soldier life/duty
- Women
- Blacks
- Other groups
- Memoirs/biographies
- Home front
- Post-armistice overseas activities
- Russian interventions
- Epilogue: demobilization, etc.

Center of Military History, U.S. Army, Washington, DC
The Historical Reference Branch of the Center functions as a reference collection to support the writing projects of the U.S. Army historical system. Its collection is open to patrons. The Branch also holds the Historical Manuscripts Collection, which is being used to write the official history of the U.S. Army.

Order of Battle of the United States Land Forces in the World War. 5 Vols. (1931–49. Reprint. Washington, DC: Center of Military History, 1988).

United States Army in the World War, 1917–1919. 17 Vols. (Washington, DC: Center of Military History, U.S. Army, 1988).

Liberty Memorial Museum, Kansas City, Missouri
The Liberty Memorial Museum of World War One is the only public museum in the U.S. devoted to WWI. The Museum's archives hold information on every combatant country in the war. The Museum is undergoing a renovation scheduled for completion in January 2000, and archivists are available by mail, phone, and appointment during this time. Some of the highlights of the extensive collection are:
- WWI U.S. and British unit, division, and regimental histories
- Archives of the 84th Infantry Division
- Signal Corps films
- WWI maps, photos, soldier correspondence, posters, and sheet music
- WWI oral history recordings

New York Public Library (NYPL), New York, New York
The NYPL has an extensive collection of WWI materials. Highlights include:

- WWI bibliographies
- Library subject catalog of WWI
- WWI monographs
- Regimental histories, U.S., U.K., Europe
- Trench and camp publications
- Manuscripts, including war diaries and correspondence from the front
- Printed archives and documentary sources from all participating nations
- Maps, photographs, posters, cartoons, etc.

National Guard Association Library, Washington, DC
The Library's holdings are organized by state and include regimental histories, the mobilization of the guard for WWI, rolls of honor, etc.

U.S. Secretary of War. *The Official Record of the United States' Part in the Great War: The Government Account of the Thirteen American Battles and the Army of Four Million Men* (Washington, DC, 1923). Official narratives by the Adjutant General's official register of awards of the Distinguished Service Cross and the Distinguished Service Medal.

Franks, Norman L.R. *Over the Front: A Complete Record of the Fighter Aces and Units of the United States and French Air Services, 1914–1918* (London: Grub Street, 1992).

Haulsee, W.M., F.G. Howe, and A.C. Doyle. *Soldiers of the Great War.* 3 Vols. (Washington, DC: Soldiers Record Publication Association, 1920, fiche 6051244). Vol. 1: Alabama–Maryland, Vol. 2: Massachusetts–Ohio, Vol. 3: Oklahoma–Wyoming. Lists of war dead from all states; includes many photos.

Navy and Marine Corps
The U.S. Navy was an all-volunteer service. Personnel records for navy officers separated after 1902, navy enlisted personnel discharged after 1885, marine officers separated after 1895, and marine enlisted personnel discharged after 1904 are kept at the NPRC in Saint Louis, Missouri.

U.S. Navy ships did not see battle in WWI. A squadron of battleships was stationed at Scapa Flow in north Scotland, and some were also used in convoy duty, minelaying, and troop transport. Capital ships over 8,000 tons that served in WWI were:

Battleships	Florida	Utah
New York	Delaware	*Cruisers*
Texas	Nevada	San Francisco
Wyoming	Oklahoma	Baltimore
Arkansas	Arizona	

National Archives, Washington, DC
Records of the Bureau of Naval Personnel (**RG 24**)
- Abstracts of service records of naval officers, 1829–1924 (film 1579079 ff./ M1328)
- Index to officers' correspondence jackets, 1913–25 (film 1578411 ff./ T1102); officers' personnel jackets and other records, 1900–25
- Index to Rendezvous Reports, Naval Auxiliary Service, 1917–19 (T1100), giving full name, ship assigned, enlistment date, and date detached or reassigned
- Index to Rendezvous Reports, Armed Guard Personnel, 1917–20 (T1101), giving full name, enlistment date, ship attached, dates of service, etc.
- Logs of U.S. naval ships and stations, 1801–1946. For more information, see Bradley, Claudia, Michael Kurtz, et al. *List of Logbooks of U.S. Navy Ships, Stations, and Miscellaneous Units, 1801–1947*. SL 44 (1978).
- Enlisted personnel correspondence jackets, 1904–43, discharges and desertions, 1882–1920, enlistment returns, 1846–1942
- State naval militias enrolled in the National Naval Volunteers (NNV)

The U.S. Marine Corps was also an all-volunteer service. The marines who served in France on the western front earned the nickname *Teufelhunde*, or "devil dogs," from the Germans because of their ferocious fighting in the trenches.
National Archives records of the U.S. Marine Corps (**RG 127**)
- Alphabetical card list of enlisted men, 1798–1941
- Deaths of enlisted men, 1838–1942
- Discharges of enlisted men, 1829–1927
- Casualty card lists, 1776–1945
- Muster rolls, 1798–1945 (T1118); security copy of muster rolls, 1893–1953 available only at the Marine Corps Historical Center, Washington Navy Yard
- 5th Marine Regiment correspondence, 1917–19
- Operational maps of the 4th Marine Infantry Brigade, France and Germany, 1918–19

Other National Archives Records
Office of the Chief of Naval Operations (**RG 38**)
- Operations, WWI through Korea, 1917–63
- Office of Naval Intelligence (ONI), suspected espionage cases, 1917–18, list of agents, 1917–20, ONI agents and informants residing in foreign countries, 1917–25, card file of navy personnel investigated, 1917–18, etc.
Bureau of Ships (**RG 19**)
- Index to the general photographs of the Bureau of Ships, 1914–46 (M1157)
Bureau of Medicine and Surgery (**RG 52**)

- Medical certificates and casualty lists, 1828–1939
- Navy Nurse Corps, 1908–75
- Registers of patients at naval hospitals, 1812–1929

Office of the Judge Advocate General (**RG 125**)

- Register of general courts-martial, 1909–43
- Indexes, registers, and slip records of summary courts-martial and deck courts, 1855–1930
- Commandeering and release of private vessels, 1917–19

Department of the Navy (**RG 80**)

- Civilian employees' returns, 1887–1939, lists, 1917–39, and service records, 1917–23
- Indexes and subject cards to the "secret and confidential" correspondence of the Office of the Secretary of the Navy, March 1917–July 1919 (film 1401499 ff./ M1092). Correspondence subjects include:

➢ arming of U.S. merchant ships against German submarine attack
➢ deployment of other antisubmarine measures
➢ suspected German espionage
➢ development and use of weapons
➢ improvement of radio communications
➢ personnel matters
➢ navy ship movements
➢ forwarding of mail to ships
➢ relations with the Allies and Latin American nations
➢ naval aeronautics
➢ postwar minesweeping missions
➢ meetings of the London Naval Board on Claims and the Paris Naval Board on Claims in 1919

The records include four indexes and one series of subject cards:

- Name and subject index, December 1917–March 1918: abstract of the document, name or title of writer or addressee, file number, and, frequently, date of the document; also places and subjects, except ships.
- Name and subject index, April 1918–July 1919: same as first index except it includes date of the communication at the beginning of each entry.
- Ship index, December 1917–March 1918: individual ships mentioned in the correspondence, arranged alphabetically by name or designation of vessel, including navy, commercial, and foreign-owned vessels.
- Ship index, April 1918–July 1919: continuation of the preceding ship index.
- Subject cards, March 1917–July 1919: information about each "secret and confidential" communication sent or received by the Secretary of the Navy and the Chief of Naval Operations, arranged according to 56 subject headings.

Navy Historical Center, Washington Navy Yard, Washington, DC

Materials on WWI are available in the operational archives, ships' histories branch, the photographic section, and the Navy Department Library. There are photos on-site of all U.S. Navy ships commissioned between 1800 and 1920. The Library's WWI holdings include ships' registers, cruise records, materials on Britain's Royal Navy, published official histories from most countries, and books on individual U.S. states in WWI.

The Operational Archives have material in the Early Records Collection on WWI naval activity, including convoy and Merchant Marine (ZO series, box 9), the Nurse Corps (ZV series, box 8), German POWs in Georgia (ZV series, box 9), the naval detachment in Turkish waters, 1919–24 (ZO series, box 2), the occupation of Germany, 1918–22 (ZO series, box 10), and other subjects.

Marine Corps Historical Center, Washington Navy Yard, Washington, DC

The Center has an oral history collection relating to WWI. They also hold WWI diaries, photographs, and operational records, including muster rolls, 1807–1949.

Frothingham, Thomas G. *The Naval History of the World War: The United States in the War, 1917–1918* (Cambridge: Harvard University Press, 1926).

Hilliard, Jack B. *An Annotated Bibliography of the United States Marine Corps in the First World War* (Washington, DC: Marine Corps Historical Division, 1967).

McClellan, Edwin N. *The United States Marine Corps in the World War* (Washington, DC: Marine Corps Historical Division, 1920).

Officers and Enlisted Men of the United States Navy Who Lost Their Lives During the World War: From April 6, 1917 to November 11, 1918 (Washington, DC: USGPO, 1920. Reprint. Fairfield, CA: Solano County Researchers, 1989, film 1415261).

Coast Guard

The Coast Guard was established in 28 January 1915 under the Treasury Department, merging the Revenue Cutter Service and the Life Saving Service. From 1917 to 1918 the Coast Guard functioned as part of the U.S. Navy. Personnel records for Coast Guard officers separated after 1928 and enlisted personnel discharged after 1914 are at the National Personnel Records Center in Saint Louis, Missouri.

National Archives, Washington, DC
Records of the U.S. Coast Guard (**RG 26**)
- Muster rolls, 1833–1932 (records prior to 1915 are of the Revenue Cutter Service)
- Officers' records, 1791–1919 (records before 1915 are of the Life Saving Service)
- Honorable discharges, 1917–19
- Personnel and pay cards, 1917–21
- Officer personnel files, 1915–29
- General and summary courts-martial, 1906–41
- Watch books, 1914–23
- Vessel logbooks, 1915–47
- Casualty and wreck reports, 1913–36 (T925–6)
- Station reports of assistance, 1917–35 (T921)
- Reports of assistance to individuals and vessels, 1916–40 (T720)

Coast Guard Historian's Office, Washington, DC
The Office maintains a card file of officers' assignments and a supplementary file on all personnel, 1915–89. There is also a large photo collection dating from 1850. There is a complete set of the *Register of Officers*, published annually.

Merchant Marine
Records of the Bureau of Marine Inspection and Navigation (**RG 41**)
- List of merchant seamen lost in WWI, 1914–19
- Recruit enrollment cards, 1918–19, applications, 1918–21
- Applications to serve on merchant vessels, 1918–19
- Seamen's protection certificates, 1918–19
- Certificates issued to lifeboatmen and able seamen, 1915–36
- List of officers licensed, 1894–1942
- U.S. Shipping Board recruit enrollment cards, 1918–19
- U.S. Shipping Board applications, 1918–21
- U.S. Shipping Board honorable and dishonorable discharges, 1917–21
Records of the U.S. Coast Guard (**RG 26**)
- Merchant Marine logbooks

Other National Archives records relating to WWI
Records of the Department of State (**RG 59**)
- Records relating to WWI and its termination, 1914–29 (M367)
Records of the War Industries Board (**RG 61**)
- Minutes, 1917–18 (M1073)
Records of the Council of National Defense (**RG 62**)

- Minutes, 1916–21 (M1069)
- Minutes, Committee on Women's Defense Work, 1917–19, subject card indexes (M1074)

Records of the Immigration and Naturalization Service (**RG 85**)

- Indexes to naturalizations of WWI solders, 1918 (T458)

Records of the Federal Bureau of Investigation (**RG 65**)

- "Old German Files," 1915–21 (M1085)

Records of the War Department and Special Staffs (**RG 165**)

- Army War College: transcripts of British, French, German, and Italian records relating to WWI, with indexes, 1917–19 (RG 165.7.2, filmed, no microcopy number)

Collection of Foreign Records Seized (**RG 242**)[14]

- German Foreign Ministry Archives, 1867–1920 (T149)
- German Armed Forces High Command, 1914–45 (T77)
- German Navy High Command, selected records, including U-boat operations, 1914–18 (T1022)
- Prussian mobilization records, 1866–1918 (M962)
- Miscellaneous records (seized in 1945), 1815–1945: Bulgarian, Croatian, Czechoslovakian, Danish, Dutch, English, Estonian, Finnish, French, Greek, Hungarian, Japanese, Latvian, Lithuanian, Romanian, Serbian, Slovenian, Turkish, and Wendish (RG 242.22)

Both Archives I in Washington, DC and Archives II in College Park, Maryland hold record groups pertaining to WWI. Some RGs (record groups) have been divided between the two repositories. It is always a good idea to check with the Textual Reference Branch before a visit, especially if the records have not been filmed.

➢ *Cited RGs at Archives I*: 15, 24, 26, 41, 52, 61, 62, 80, 85, 92, 117, 120, 125, 127, 153, 165, 231, 391, 392, 393, 395, 407

➢ *Cited RGs at Archives II*: 18, 19, 38, 59, 65, 90, 242

Burial Records

Aside from those individuals buried in private cemeteries, three agencies maintain cemeteries and burial records for military personnel and veterans.

American Battle Monuments Commission, Washington, DC

The Commission maintains American military burial grounds on foreign soil.

---

[14] RG 242 is available at Archives II, College Park.

They provide free information to families and friends of all who are interred in these cemeteries. Records are also available at the National Archives (**RG 117**).

The Commission maintains the following WWI cemeteries:
France: Aisne-Marne, Bellicourt Monument, Chateau-Thierry Monument, Meuse-Argonne, Montfaucon Monument, Montsec Monument, Naval Monument at Brest, Oise-Aisne, Saint-Mihiel, Somme, Sommepy Monument, Surenes, Tours Monument. *Belgium*: Audernarde Monument, Flanders Field. *England*: Brookwood, and the Naval Monument at *Gibraltar*. For more information, see:

- American Battle Monuments Commission. *Summary of Operations in the World War*. 28 Vols. (Washington, DC: The Commission, 1944, **RG 117**). Plotted maps showing the front line position of each AEF division, accompanied by narratives.
- Nishiura, Elizabeth. *American Battle Monuments: A Guide to Military Cemeteries and Monuments Maintained by the American Battle Monuments Commission* (Detroit: Omnigraphics, 1989).
- American Battle Monuments Commission. *Armies and Battlefields in Europe* (Washington, DC: USGPO, 1938. Reprint. Washington, DC: Center of Military History, 1992).

Department of Veterans' Affairs, National Cemetery System, Washington, DC

The System oversees and maintains 113 national cemeteries and has custody of more than two million burial records; it keeps a card file index, 1861 to the present, for all cemeteries. To examine the benefit file of a deceased veteran, a member of the immediate family must submit a written application to the local Department office and include: full name of veteran, branch of service, and service number or Social Security number.

WWI Graves Registration Service (GRS)

The GRS was formed in August 1917, but did not deploy to Europe until October. Much of the initial work was done by the Army Quartermaster Corps, which absorbed the GRS in 1920. The graves were in England, Belgium, France, Germany, Italy, Luxembourg, and Murmansk, Russia. All the remains in Germany, Luxembourg, and Russia were relocated to France or returned to the United States.

Records of the Office of Quartermaster General (**RG 92**)
Graves Registration Service
- Burial reports, 1918–19
- Burial registers and cemetery lists, 1917–22

- Disinterments and reburials, 1919–31
- Gold Star mothers' and widows' pilgrimage to Europe, 1930–3; see also *Pilgrimage for Mothers and Widows of Soldiers, Sailors, and Marines of the American Forces Now Interred in the Cemeteries of Europe* (Washington, DC: USGPO, 1930).

Memorial Division

- Headstone applications, 1909–62; army combatants only through 1948, after that time all U.S. forces, deceased in service or honorably discharged
- Burial case files, 1915–39
- Burial registers, 1862–1918
- Records of cemeteries at abandoned army posts, 1874–1947

Arlington National Cemetery, Arlington, Virginia

Arlington is under the auspices of the Department of the Army, and its records are not included in the Department of Veterans' Affairs. There is a card index on site that the staff can search by surname or Social Security number.

Holt, Dean W. *American Military Cemeteries: A Comprehensive Illustrated Guide to the Hallowed Grounds of the United States, Including Cemeteries Overseas* (Jefferson, NC: McFarland and Co., 1992).

Soldiers' and Sailors' Homes and Hospitals

From 1866 to 1930 the National Homes for Disabled Volunteer Soldiers were authorized by Congress. In 1930 they were consolidated into the Veterans' Administration. Records are under the Veterans' Administration (**RG 15**) and include:

- Registers for the homes, 1866–1937 (film 1536167 ff.), including homes in California, Illinois, Indiana, Kansas, Maine, New York, Ohio, Oregon, South Dakota, Tennessee, Virginia, and Wisconsin

Records of the U.S. Soldiers' Home in Washington, DC (**RG 231**). Accepted army personnel only until 1917, also accepted Army Air Force personnel from that time until 1947.

- Registers of men admitted and discharged, 1851–1841
- Registers of sick inmates, 1872–1943
- Records of deceased inmates, 1852–1942

U.S. Naval Home, Philadelphia (**RG 24.8.1**)

- Station logs, 1842–1942

U.S. Naval Hospital, Philadelphia (**RG 24.8.2**)

- Admissions and discharges, 1867–1917

U.S. Naval Hospital, Brooklyn, New York (**RG 52.4.2**)

- Register of remains of military personnel returned from Europe, 1919–22

Public Health Service (**RG 90**)
* Reports of patients admitted and discharged at Marine and Public Health Hospitals, 1877–1920
* Records of hospitals and field medical installations, 1794–1944

Another source for death records is the Social Security Death Index, available on CD-ROM at Family History Centers and also commercially for individual purchase. If a WWI veteran had a Social Security number and died after 1962, he may be in the Index. The present version contains 53.5 million records but is not complete from 1962. Newspaper obituaries are also a good place to search, particularly local papers.

VFW Locator Service

The Veterans of Foreign Wars (VFW) offers a fee-based veteran locator service. They provide a list of matching names and military history. The fee is refunded if no match can be found. Contact:

Vets National Archives, Finders/Seekers

1809 Vandiver Drive

Columbia, MO 65202-1916

American Volunteers in WWI
American Red Cross Archives, Alexandria, Virginia
This is the official archive for the American Red Cross. The records for 1881 to 1946 have been transferred to the National Archives; these records must still be requested through the Red Cross Archives and transferred to their location for examination. These records apply to all branches of the armed forces.
* Red Cross personnel records, surname index for WWI
* Casualty and POW index for WWI
* Place index for WWI
* Event index for WWI
* Photograph collection of WWI

YMCA of the USA Archives, University of Minnesota Library, Saint Paul, Minnesota
* Records for the Young Mens' Christian Association, including those who served with the YMCA in WWI
* YMCA historical records of WWI

Hoover Institution, Stanford University, Stanford, California
* American Library Association War Service, records, 1917–23

- Materials on the American Volunteer Motor Ambulance Corps in France, Albania, the Balkans, and Italy
- Materials on American volunteers in the Serbian army
- American Relief Administration activities in Belgium, Romania, Trans-Caucasia, and Upper Silesia
- YMCA activities in Austria, Russia, and Siberia
- American Red Cross activities in the Balkans, China, Italy, the Middle East, Poland, and Siberia
- Society of Friends War Victims Relief Committee, records, 1914–23, for Austria, France, Germany, and Hungary
- Christian Science War Relief Depot, Le Mans, France, miscellaneous records, 1918–19

American Field Service Archives and Museum, New York, New York
- Drivers' journals, diaries, and personal collections, 1914–56
- Section histories and historical reports, December 1914–December 1916
- *History of the American Field Service in France, Friends of France, 1914–1917: Told by its Members*. 3 Vols. (Boston: Houghton Mifflin Co., 1920).
- Geller, L.D. *The American Field Service Archives of World War I, 1914–1917* (Westport CT: Greenwood Press, 1989).

Addresses

National Archives (Archives I)
700 Pennsylvania Avenue NW
Washington, DC 20408

*National Archives at College Park
(Archives II)*
8601 Adelphi Road
College Park, MD 20740-6001

*National Personnel Records
Center*
Military Records Facility
9700 Page Avenue
Saint Louis, MO 63132-5100

*U.S. Army Military History
Institute*
22 Asburn Drive
Carlisle Barracks, PA 17013-5008

Center of Military History
Historical Resources Branch
1099 14th Street NW
Washington, DC 20005-3402

Liberty Memorial Museum
100 West 26th Street
Kansas City, MO 64108

New York Public Library
5th Avenue and 42nd Street
New York, NY 10018

American Red Cross Archives
Hazel Braugh Records Center
5818 Seminary Road
Alexandria, VA 22041

Navy Historical Center
Washington Navy Yard
Building 44
901 M Street SE
Washington, DC 20374-5060

Marine Corps Historical Center
Washington Navy Yard
Building 58
901 M Street SE
Washington, DC 20374-5060

Coast Guard Historian's Office
2100 Second Street SW
Washington, DC 20593

American Battle Monuments Commission
Casimir Pulaski Building
20 Massachusetts Avenue NW
Washington, DC 20314-0300

National Cemetery System
Department of Veterans' Affairs
810 Vermont Avenue NW
Washington, DC 20420

Arlington National Cemetery
Superintendent
Arlington, VA 22211

National Guard Association Library
1 Massachusetts Avenue NW
Washington, DC 20001

Hoover Institution Archives
Stanford University
Stanford, CA 94305-6010

Army Pentagon Library
6605 Army Pentagon
Washington, DC 20310

American Merchant Marine Veterans
4720 SE 15th Avenue
Cape Coral, FL 33904-9600

Records Organized by State

Most state historical societies, archives, or libraries have information regarding WWI veterans who enlisted from that particular state. Most often found are casualty lists, "Gold Star" lists and Rolls of Honor; statements of service; discharge records; copies of Selective Service records; regimental and unit histories; and financial aid to veterans.

For most of the addresses of state offices and facilities, see Bentley, Elizabeth P. *The Genealogist's Address Book.* 3rd ed. (Baltimore: Genealogical Publishing Co., 1995, or current edition). For addresses of regional offices of the Department of Veterans' Affairs, or National Guard State Adjutant General's offices, see Johnson, Richard S. *How to Locate Anyone Who is or Ever Has Been in the Military.* 7th ed. (Spartanburg, NC: MIE Publishing, 1996).

There was no federal pension paid to veterans of WWI, but some states issued what were called "bonuses," or paid claims, provided relief, and issued loans.

The states that had a bonus program were Illinois, Kansas, Kentucky, Louisiana, Maine, Massachusetts, Michigan, Minnesota, Missouri, New Jersey, Oregon, South Dakota, Washington, and Wisconsin. Pennsylvania and Ohio had a compensation fund, North Carolina instituted a loan fund, Louisiana issued pensions (in addition to bonuses), and Maine had a relief commission for disabled veterans (in addition to bonuses).

Counties in some states also kept military records, usually relating to discharges, but also including service records, honor rolls, and copies of Selective Service records. *Examples* of some of the categories to look for in county records are:
➢ *Register of deeds*: discharge records, i.e., Kansas and Illinois
➢ *County clerk or recorder*: rolls and discharge records, i.e., South Carolina, New York, Illinois, California
➢ *County court*: service records and discharges, i.e., Oklahoma, Tennessee, Texas, Georgia

Military petitions for naturalization can be found in county, state, and federal court records, especially when they were in proximity to a military or naval installation. During WWI entire busloads of recruits were often driven to the local courthouse to become citizens. The naturalization law of 1918 provided that aliens serving in U.S. forces in WWI could be naturalized without any residency requirement (40 Stat. 542 § 1). [15]

Alabama
Selective Service draft registration cards, 1917–18 (film 1509347 ff./ M1509)
Alabama Department of Archives and History, Montgomery
• WWI service records, 1918–19 (film 1644084 ff.), card rosters of personnel
• Directories of personnel, 1915–18
• Roll of Honor
• Casualty list
Military Police Corps Regimental Museum, Fort McClennan
• Regimental histories of the Police Corps
• WWI maps and photos, genealogical material

Alaska
Selective Service draft registration cards, 1917–18 (film 1473296 ff./ M1509)

Banks, Raymond. *The Banks Compilation of Birth Data of Men with Links to Alaska Territory Who Were Born 1873–1900: As Found in the Civilian*

---

[15] Christina K. Schaefer, *Guide to Naturalization Records of the United States* (Baltimore: Genealogical Publishing Co., 1997), 5.

Registration Cards [World War I Selective Service Draft Registration Cards] (Salt Lake City: The Author, 1996).

Arizona
Selective Service draft registration cards, 1917–18 (film 1473300 ff./ M1509)
Department of Library, Archives, and Public Records, Phoenix
• List of POWs from Arizona

Arkansas
Selective Service draft registration cards, 1917–18 (film 1522740 ff./ M1509)
Arkansas History Commission, Little Rock
• Selective Service registrations
• WWI nurses from Arkansas
• Discharge records
• County discharge records on microfilm

California
Selective Service draft registration cards, 1917–18 (film 1530652 ff./ M1509)
California State Archives, Sacramento
• Adjutant General's WWI draft report of California men who enlisted or were inducted into the army, navy, or marines (film 0002496).
• Records of the California National Guard in WWI

Colorado
Selective Service draft registration cards, 1917–18 (film 1544462 ff./ M1509)
Colorado State Archives, Denver
• Colorado WWI veterans, deceased

Connecticut
Selective Service draft registration cards, 1917–18 (film 1561876 ff./ M1509)
Connecticut State Library, Hartford
• Statements of service and service certificates, 1919–44
• Selective Service correspondence, registrations, inductions
• Recipients of the Distinguished Service Cross, 1918
• Memorial certificates issued to next of kin
• WWI Roll of Honor
• Military census of Connecticut, 1919–20 (film 1530633 ff.), enumeration of all males over age 16, and nurses
Company of Military Historians, Westbrook
• Reference library including general titles, WWI, and videos
• Information network of other military history institutions, both nationally and internationally, that are members of the Company

- Referrals to members who have expertise in particular aspects of military history
- Special collection on women in the military

Connecticut Adjutant General's Office. *Connecticut Service Records: Men and Women in the Armed Forces of the United States During the World War, 1917–1920.* 3 Vols. (Hartford: Office of the Adjutant General, 1941).

Delaware
Selective Service draft registration cards, 1917–18 (film 1570621 ff./ M1509)
Hall of Records, Dover
- Selective Service inductions
- Roll of Honor, 1918–21
- WWI statements of service, navy
- Card index of Delaware soldiers and sailors in WWI
- First Delaware Infantry muster-in roll, 1917

District of Columbia
Selective Service draft registration cards, 1917–18 (film 1570933 ff./ M1509)

Florida
Selective Service draft registration cards, 1917–18 (film 1556849 ff./ M1509)
Florida State Archives, Tallahassee
- WWI navy card roster, 1917–20 (film 1672940 ff.), Florida Adjutant General's Office
- WWI Coast Guard and marine roster, 1917–19
- Selective Service inductions
- WPA grave registration cards of Florida veterans

Georgia
Selective Service draft registration cards, 1917–18 (film 1556940 ff./ M1509)
Georgia Department of Archives and History, Atlanta
- WWI statements of service
- WWI service record abstracts
- Georgia National Guard register, 1915–17 (before federalization)
- Applications for the Victory Medal, and service medals issued
- Honor Roll
Boss, Bert E. *The Georgia State Memorial Book* (n.p.: American Memorial Publishing Co., 1921, film 0175271).

Hawaii
Selective Service draft registration cards, 1917–18 (film 1452025 ff./ M1509)

Hawaii State Archives, Honolulu
*   Hawaii WWI veterans, deceased
*   2nd Hawaiian Infantry muster-in roll, 1918
*   WWI statements of service, 1915–21, army
*   WWI statements of service, 1915–21, navy
*   Hawaiian National Guard records, 1914–18

Kuykendall, Ralph Simpson. *Hawaii in the World War* (Honolulu: Historical Commission, 1928, film 1321393).

Idaho
Selective Service draft registration cards, 1917–18 (film 1452106 ff./ M1509)
Idaho State Historical Society, Bosie
*   Selective Service registrations and inductions

Idaho Adjutant General. *Biennial Report, 1917–1918* (Boise: Office of the Adjutant General, 1919).

Illinois
Selective Service draft registration cards, 1917–18 (film 1452428 ff./ M1509)
Illinois State Archives, Springfield
*   Selective Service registrations
*   Bonus applications and payment vouchers
Department of Veterans' Affairs, Springfield
*   WPA graves registration of veterans

Fighting Men of Illinois (Chicago: Publishers Subscription Co., 1918, film 0934978).

Indiana
Selective Service draft registration cards, 1917–18 (film 1439777 ff./ M1509)
Indiana State Archives, Indianapolis
*   Selective Service registrations, 1917–18 (film 1674855 ff.)
*   Indiana nurses' enrollment cards (film 1683687). Full name, residence, birth date and place, appointment date to nurse, promotions, organizations, staff assignments, engagements, wounds received, overseas service, remarks, date of discharge.
*   Gold Star Honor Roll, 1914–18

Gold Star Honor Roll: A Record of Indiana Men and Women Who Died in the Service of the United States and the Allied Nations in the World War, 1914–1918 (Indianapolis: Indiana Historical Commission, 1921, film 1673274).

Iowa
Selective Service draft registration cards, 1917–18 (film 1642846 ff./ M1509)
State Historical Society of Iowa, Des Moines
• WWI casualty file
Department of Veterans' Affairs, Des Moines
• Adjutant General records of the Iowa National Guard in WWI

Kansas
Selective Service draft registration cards, 1917–18 (film 1643420 ff./ M1509)
Kansas State Historical Society, Topeka
• Selective Service registrations and inductions
• Kansas State Guard commissions, 1917
• First Kansas Cavalry muster-in roll, 1917
• 117th Ammunition Train, Rainbow Division, roster, 1917–18
• Casualty list
• Bonus applications, with enlistment and discharge records
• Kansas veterans buried in France
Federal Archives and Records Center, Kansas City, Missouri
• U.S. Bureau of Indian Affairs, Potawatomi Agency. Records of Native Americans in WWI, Potawatomi and Kickapoo tribes (film 1015903).

Kentucky
Selective Service draft registration cards, 1917–18 (film 1643933 ff./ M1509)
Kentucky Department of Military Affairs, Frankfort
• Kentucky State Guard muster-in rolls
• Selective Service inductions
• Bonus applications
• Casualty lists
• POWs from Kentucky

Index to Veterans of American Wars from Kentucky (Frankfort: Kentucky Historical Society, 1966, film 0471728 ff.).

Louisiana
Selective Service draft registration cards, 1917–18 (film 1653576 ff./ M1509)
Louisiana State Archives, Baton Rouge
• Bonuses and pensions issued to WWI veterans and widows
• List of WWI officers and soldiers from Louisiana

Historical Records Survey. *Inventory of the Records of World War Emergency Activities in Louisiana, 1916–1920* (Baton Rouge: Louisiana State University, 1942, film 0908038).

Maine

Selective Service draft registration cards, 1917–18 (film 1653898 ff./ M1509)
Maine State Archives, Augusta
- Selective Service registrations
- Bonus applications and receipts
- Applications for the Victory Medal
- Relief Commission records
- Discharge records, 1914–22
- Maine Adjutant General records
- Honor Roll
- Maine women in WWI

Maine Adjutant General. *Roster of Maine in the Military Service of the United States and Allies in the World War, 1917–1919.* 2 Vols. (Augusta: James W. Hanson, the Adjutant General, 1929, film 1036025 ff.). Includes records of the army and navy nurse corps.

Maryland

Selective Service draft registration cards, 1917–18 (film 1654024 ff./ M1509)
Maryland State Archives, Annapolis
- Maryland Adjutant General, militia enrollment and muster-in rolls, 1917

Maryland in the World War, 1917–1919: Military and Naval Service Records. 2 Vols. (Baltimore: Maryland War Records Commission, 1933, film 1670787).

Massachusetts

Selective Service draft registration cards, 1917–18 (film 1684875 ff./ M1509)
Massachusetts State Archives, Boston
- Bonus applications and records
Military Archives and Museum, Worcester Armory, Worcester
- U.S. Army, Massachusetts Infantry, casualties from Massachusetts, 1918 (film 1544205 ff.).
- Massachusetts State Guard records, 1917–20
- Casualty lists
- Selective Service registrations, inductions, and delinquents; records filmed for the Local Board, Division 43 (Barnstable), exemptions as aliens, 1917–18 (film 1846563).
- Statements of service
- Discharge records
- Lists of army POWs from Massachusetts
- Massachusetts 26th Division, sailing list, 1917

Michigan
Selective Service draft registration cards, 1917–18 (film 1675112 ff./ M1509)
State Archives of Michigan, Lansing
- Index of deserters from draft, 1917–18 (film 1765776 ff.)
- WWI card index for Michigan (film 1001930 ff.)
- Bonus applications
- Michigan muster-in rolls, 1917
- Applications for the Victory Medal
- Roll of Honor, 1917–19

Minnesota
Selective Service draft registration cards, 1917–18 (film 1675275 ff./ M1509)
Minnesota Historical Society, Saint Paul
- Selective Service registrations
- Bonus applications and records

Holbrook, Franklin F. and Livia Appel. *Minnesota in the War with Germany.* 2 Vols. (Saint Paul: Minnesota Historical Society, 1932).

Mississippi
Selective Service draft registration cards, 1917–18 (film 1682699 ff./ M1509)
Mississippi Department of Archives and History, Jackson
- WWI army veterans index, 1917–18 (film 0904445 ff.).
- Honor Roll

Missouri
Selective Service draft registration cards, 1917–18 (film 1683089 ff./ M1509)
Department of Veterans' Affairs, Jefferson City
- Statements of service, Missouri Adjutant General
- Bonus application papers

Raupp, William A. *Report of the Adjutant General of Missouri, January 10, 1921–December 31, 1924* (Jefferson City: Hugh Stephens, 1925, fiche 6125619). Includes Missouri roster of WWI casualties for the army, navy, marines, National Guard and army nurses; lists of veterans for the regular U.S. Army and National Guard.

Montana
Selective Service draft registration cards, 1917–18 (film 1684099 ff./ M1509)
Montana Historical Society, Helena
- Montana veterans of WWI, card file
- WWI service records

- Montana National Guard enlistments, 1905–20

Nebraska
Selective Service draft registration cards, 1917–18 (film 1684016 ff./ M1509)
Nebraska State Historical Society, Lincoln
- Selective Service registrations
- Nebraska veterans service cards
- Nebraska Home Guard files, 1917–19

Nebraska Secretary of State. *Roster of Soldiers, Sailors, and Marines Who Served in the War of the Rebellion, Spanish-American War, and World War* (Omaha: Waters-Barnhart Printing Co., 1925).

Nevada
Selective Service draft registration cards, 1917–18 (film 1711534 ff./ M1509)
Nevada State Library and Archives, Carson City
- Selective Service registrations
- Nevada veterans service cards
- Discharge records
- Gold Star Honor Roll

Sullivan, Maurice J., Adjutant General. *Nevada's Golden Stars: A Memorial Volume Designed as a Gift from the State of Nevada to the Relatives of Those Nevada Heroes Who Died in the World War* (Reno: A. Carlisle, 1924. Reprint. Tucson: W.C. Cox, 1974, film 1000195).

New Hampshire
Selective Service draft registration cards, 1917–18 (film 1711715 ff./ M1509)
New Hampshire State Archives, Concord
- Selective Service registrations
- New Hampshire National Guard officers' roster

New Jersey
Selective Service draft registration cards, 1917–18 (film 1711811 ff./ M1509)
New Jersey State Archives, Trenton
- New Jersey National Guard and State Militia muster-in rolls, 1917
- Bonus records
- Partial service records, 1917–18

New Mexico
Selective Service draft registration cards, 1917–18 (film 1711857 ff./ M1509)
New Mexico Records Center and Archives, Santa Fe

- Selective Service inductions
- "Veterans Service Records" forms, 1919–20
- Casualty lists
- Discharge records

New York
Selective Service draft registration cards, 1917–18 (film 1711815 ff./ M1509)
New York State Archives, Albany
- New York veterans of WWI, card catalog
- New York National Guard and Naval Militia service record abstracts

Century Association. *Record of Service Rendered in the Great War* (New York: DeVinne Press, 1920).

New York Adjutant General. *Citizens of the State of New York Who Died while in Service of the United States During the World War* (Albany: J.B. Lyon Co., 1922).

A Spirit of Sacrifice, New York's Response to the Great War: A Guide to Records Relating to World War I Held in the New York State Archives (Albany: State Archives and Records, 1993).

North Carolina
Selective Service draft registration cards, 1917–18 (film 1765557 ff./ M1509)
North Carolina State Archives, Raleigh
- Selective Service inductions
- North Carolina National Guard rosters
- Certificates of service, 1917–18
- Roll of Honor
- WWI Loan Fund
- WPA graves index, post-1914

Military Personnel Records in the North Carolina State Archives, 1918–64 (Raleigh: The Archives, 1973).

North Carolina Adjutant General. *Annual Reports, 1917–1918* (Raleigh: Edwards and Broughton, 1920).

Lemmon, Sarah, M. *North Carolina's Role in the First World War* (Raleigh: North Carolina Division of Archives and History, 1975).

North Dakota

Selective Service draft registration cards, 1917–18 (film 1819402 ff./ M1509)
State Historical Society of North Dakota, Bismarck
*   Selective Service inductions

Fraser, Angus, North Dakota Adjutant General. *Roster of Men and Women Who Served in the Army or Naval Services (Including Marine Corps) of the United States or Its Allies from the State of North Dakota in the World War, 1917–1918.* 4 Vols. (Bismarck: Bismarck Tribune Co., 1931, film 0982257 ff.).

Ohio

Selective Service draft registration cards, 1917–18 (film 1819504 ff./ M1509)
Ohio Historical Society, Columbus
*   Certificates of service, 1917–20
*   Compensation Fund claims and warrants
Division of Veterans' Affairs, Columbus
*   Marine Corps service cards (film 0195436 ff.)
*   Navy service cards (film 0195439 ff.)
*   Out-of-state service cards (film 0195447 ff.).
*   Service cards of the state of Ohio (film 0195337 ff.)
*   Ohio National Guard, commissioned officers, 1890–1917 (film 0195464)

Ohio Adjutant General. *The Official Roster of Ohio Soldiers, Sailors, and Marines in the World War, 1917–1918.* 22 Vols. (Columbus: F.J. Heer Printing Co., 1926–9, film 0195413 ff.).

Oklahoma

Selective Service draft registration cards, 1917–18 (film 1851604 ff./ M1509)
Office of Archives and Records, Oklahoma City
*   Roll of Honor
*   Oklahoma veterans buried in Europe

Hoffmann, Roy. *Oklahoma Honor Roll, World War I, 1917–1918* (Oklahoma City: The Author, n.d.).

Daugherty, Fred. *Oklahoma Citizen-Soldier Organizations: Their Participation in the Wars of Our Country* (Oklahoma City: 45th Infantry Division Museum, 1991).

Oregon

Selective Service draft registration cards, 1917–18 (film 1851979 ff./ M1509)
Oregon State Archives, Salem

- Selective Service inductions
- Bonus applications and records
- Service records, 1847–1920
- Unit records, 1917–48, rosters, 1865–1939
- Oregon National Guard records through 1920
- State Historian of the Defense Council, WWI biographical questionnaires

Pennsylvania
Selective Service draft registration cards, 1917–18 (film 1852246 ff./ M1509)
Pennsylvania State Archives, Harrisburg
- Selective Service registrations and inductions
- Pennsylvania National Guard muster-in rolls, 1917
- Discharge certificates
- Veterans' compensation applications
- Card index of Pennsylvania volunteers in the navy
Pennsylvania Military History Museum, Boalsburg
- Maps, published histories
- Genealogical materials relating to WWI

Pennsylvania State Publications Society. *Pennsylvanians in the World War: An Illustrated History of the Twenty-Eighth Division . . .* 2 Vols. (Pittsburgh: The Society, 1921).

Rhode Island
Selective Service draft registration cards, 1917–18 (film 1852212 ff./ M1509)
Rhode Island State Archives, Providence
- Selective Service registrations
- Discharge records

South Carolina
Selective Service draft registration cards, 1917–18 (film 1852489 ff./ M1509)
South Carolina Department of Archives and History, Columbia
- Selective Service inductions
- Adjutant General's records of enlistments and service statements
- Applications for the Victory Medal
- Officers' record cards, 1878–1921
- Casualty lists
Florence Air and Missile Museum, Florence
- Air Corps pilots in WWI
- Lafayette Escadrille collection

South Carolina Adjutant General. *The Official Roster of South Carolina*

Soldiers, Sailors, and Marines in the World War, 1917–1918. 2 Vols. (Columbia: Office of the Adjutant General, 1932).

South Dakota
Selective Service draft registration cards, 1917–18 (film 1877785 ff./ M1509)
South Dakota Historical Society, South Dakota Archives, Pierre
- WPA graves registration of veterans
- Bonus applications and payments
- Mothers' pensions, 1913–40

Hanson, Joseph M. *South Dakota in the World War, 1917–1919* (Pierre: State Historical Society, 1940).

Tennessee
Selective Service draft registration cards, 1917–18 (film 1852852 ff./ M1509)
Tennessee State Library and Archives, Nashville
- Selective Service inductions
- Gold Star Honor Roll
- Tennessee WWI veterans file

Texas
Selective Service draft registration cards, 1917–18 (film 1927189 ff./ M1509)
Texas State Library and Archives, Austin
- WPA graves registration of veterans
First Cavalry Division Museum, Fort Hood
- WWI unit histories
- WWI after-action reports
- History of the 1st Cavalry Division

White, Lonnie J. *The 90th Division in World War I: The Texas-Oklahoma Draft Division in the Great War* (Texas: Sunflower University, 1996).

Utah
Selective Service draft registration cards, 1917–18 (film 1983881 ff./ M1509)
Utah State Archives and Records Service, Salt Lake City
- Selective Service draft board registrations, 1917–18 (film 1666078 ff.), of local draft board registers of counties throughout Utah
- Statements of service, Utah WWI veterans
- Service questionnaires compiled by Utah WWI veterans (film 0485733 ff.)
- Discharge records

Warrum, Noble. *Utah in the World War: The Men Behind the Guns and the Men and Women Behind the Men Behind the Guns* (Salt Lake City: Utah State Council of Defense, 1924, film 1033897).

Vermont

Selective Service draft registration cards, 1917–18 (film 1984059 ff./ M1509)
Department of Veterans' Affairs, Office of the Adjutant General, Montpelier
- Vermont National Guard muster-in rolls, 1917
- WPA graves registration of veterans

Johnson, Herbert, Adjutant General. *Roster of Vermont Men and Women in the Military and Naval Service of the United States and Allies in the World War, 1917–1919* (Rutland: Tuttle Co., 1927).

Virginia

Selective Service draft registration cards, 1917–18 (film 1984203 ff./ M1509)
Virginia State Library and Archives, Richmond
- Selective Service inductions
- WWI History Commission files, 1919–20
Army Transportation Museum, Fort Eustis
- Army Tank Corps collection from 1914
- Reference works, personal papers, photos
War Memorial Museum of Virginia, Newport News
- WWI maps, photos, artifacts, weapons, uniforms, etc.
George C. Marshall Research Foundation and Library, Virginia Military Institute, Lexington
- WWI regimental histories
- Operational reports
- Signal Corps photos
- Maps, personal papers

Virginia Military Organizations in the World War, with Supplement of Distinguished Service (Richmond: n.p., 1927).

Washington

Selective Service draft registration cards, 1917–18 (film 1991532 ff./ M1509)
Washington State Archives, Olympia
- Washington National Guard service cards
- Bonus applications
Washington National Guard Historical Office, Tacoma
- WWI personnel files
- WWI unit histories

Washington National Guard Pamphlet: The Official History of the Washington National Guard. 3 Vols. (Tacoma: Office of the Adjutant General, 1961, film 1321447).

West Virginia
Selective Service draft registration cards, 1917–18 (film 1992327 ff./ M1509)
Archives and History Library, Charleston
• Statements of service, West Virginia WWI veterans
• WPA casualties index
Office of the Adjutant General for West Virginia, Charleston
• Selective Service inductions
• Applications for the Victory Medal
• Records of the West Virginia National Guard in WWI

Wisconsin
Selective Service draft registration cards, 1917–18 (film 1685061 ff./ M1509)
State Historical Society of Wisconsin, Madison
• Selective Service draft registrations, 1917 (film 1728222 ff.)
• Wisconsin State Guard in WWI
• Bonus applications and payments
• Gold Star Honor Roll
Wisconsin Veterans Historical Museum, Madison
• Military history of Wisconsin veterans
• Manuscripts, letters, maps, photos, etc.

Gregory, John G. *Wisconsin's Gold Star List: Soldiers, Sailors, Marines, and Nurses from the Badger State Who Served in the World War* (Madison: State Historical Society, 1925, fiche 6051352).

Wyoming
Selective Service draft registration cards, 1917–18 (film 1993029 ff./ M1509)
Wyoming State Archives, Cheyenne
• Selective Service registrations
• Casualty list
• Discharge records

Puerto Rico
Selective Service draft registration cards 1917–18 (film 2022911 ff./ M1509)

The Philippines
The Philippine Islands were a territory of the U.S. in 1914. During the war some Filipinos served in the U.S. Army. A national guard was raised in the Philippines

for the duration of the war. There was no standing army at the time of WWI, but conscription enrollment was practiced for the Philippines Constabulary.
Record Management and Archives Office, Manila

- *Qunitas* (conscription lists), 1860–1919 (film 1716896)
- Philippines National Guard. Service records, 1917–19 (film 1681483 ff.). A series of index cards gives the name, rank, company, and province in which the recruit enlisted.

Suggested Reading

Coffman, Edward M. *The War to End All Wars: The American Military Experience in World War I* (New York: Oxford University Press, 1968).

Gavin, Lettie. *American Women in World War I: They also Served* (Ninot: University Press of Colorado, 1997).

Johnson, Richard S. *How to Locate Anyone Who is or Has Been in the Military.* 7th ed. (Spartanburg, SC: MIE Press, 1996).

Kennedy, Paul M. *Over Here: The First World War and American Society* (New York: Oxford University Press, 1980).

Neagles, James C. *U.S. Military Records: A Guide to Federal and State Sources* (Salt Lake City: Ancestry Inc., 1994).

Schaffer, Ronald. *The United States in World War I: A Selected Bibliography* (Santa Barbara, CA: Clio Books, 1978).

Schneider, Dorothy and Carl J. Schneider. *Into the Breach: American Women Overseas in World War I* (New York: Viking Press, 1991).

Smith, Julia. "Somewhere in France." *Ancestry* 15 (January/February 1997): 42–5.

Thompson, Bruce D. *Military Museums, Historic Sites, and Exhibits* (Falls Church, VA: Military Living, 1992). Lists all museums for the U.S. Army, U.S. Air Force, U.S. Navy, U.S. Coast Guard, and U.S. Marine Corps, and National Park military sites and military cemeteries.

Tuchman, Barbara W. *The Zimmerman Telegram* (New York: Viking Press, 1958).

Venzon, Anne C. *The United States in the First World War: An Encyclopedia* (New York: Garland Publishing Inc., 1996).

Woodward, David R. and Robert Franklin Maddox. *America and World War I: A Selected Annotated Bibliography of English-Language Sources* (New York: Garland Publishing Inc., 1985).

15 Window in Rochester, New York home, 1917 (property of Author)

The Neutral Countries

In addition to the countries listed below, Bulgaria, Greece, Italy, Portugal, Romania, Turkey, and the U.S. were all neutral in August 1914 but entered the war at a later date.

Albania

Albania declared independence from the Ottoman Empire in 1912. Although neutral, it was occupied by both Greece and Italy. Battles between Serbian and Austro-Hungarian armies were fought within its borders. The last of the occupation troops did not leave until August 1920.

Denmark, Norway, and Sweden

In December 1914 the monarchs of the Scandinavian countries decided to maintain a neutral stance on the war. Both Sweden and Norway suffered heavy losses of merchant ships. After the Armistice, Swedish and Danish troops fought in Estonia and Finland against Russian Red forces, and Norwegian troops also fought in Finland. All three countries had some territory gain as a result of the war.

The Netherlands

Dutch neutrality was declared at the outbreak of the war. During the entire conflict, the Dutch military remained mobilized. The country's merchant shipping suffered heavy losses as a consequence of Germany's unrestricted submarine warfare.

Spain

Spain was politically divided during WWI and did not engage in combat. Its merchant fleet suffered heavy losses.

Switzerland

Traditionally a neutral country, Switzerland did mobilize its reserve forces to guard its own borders during WWI. The records for the Swiss army are at the Eidgenoessisches Militaer Department, Bundeshaus, 3000 Bern, Switzerland.

The International Red Cross in Geneva was central in monitoring the fates of prisoners of war and internees and in assisting with relief efforts.

Suggested Reading

Gomez, Carillo E. *In the Heart of the Tragedy* (London: Hodder and Stoughton,

1918).

Sweden, Norway, Denmark, and Iceland in the World War (New Haven: Yale University Press, 1930).

Frey, Marc. "Trade, Ships, and the Neutrality of the Netherlands in the First World War." *International History Review* 19 (August 1997) 3: 541–62.

Vandenbosch, A. *The Neutrality of the Netherlands during the War* (Grand Rapids, MI: Eeerdmans, 1927).

Part Three

AFTERMATH

If I should die, think only this of me:
That there's some corner of a foreign field
That is for ever England . . .
— Rupert Brooke, *1914*

16 Post-war Europe, 1920

Aftermath

COUNTRY	WAR DEATHS
Australia	62,000
Austria-Hungary	1,290,000
Belgium	44,000
Bulgaria	90,000
Canada	65,000
France	1,400,000
Germany	1,800,000
Great Britain	888,000
Greece	5,000
India	72,000
Italy	615,000
Japan	300
Montenegro	3,000
New Zealand	18,000
Newfoundland	1,000
Ottoman Empire	325,000
Portugal	7,000
Romania	335,000
Russia	1,700,000
Serbia	45,000
South Africa	9,300
United States	116,000

Casualties

Total war deaths for WWI are estimated to be more than six million, but the records for some countries were not well kept, and the actual total many be much higher. This does not account for civilian deaths. In Serbia 650,000 civilians died, and more than two million died in the Ottoman Empire (Turkey), mostly Armenians.

Influenza, 1918–1920

The Pandemic of 1918, also called the Spanish Flu, affected 20% of the world's population. The death toll from the flu was greater than from the war itself. The flu immobilized the armed forces: more than 60% of the deaths in the U.S. Army in 1918 were attributed to the flu. Total death estimates are at least 27 million.

Beveridge, William. *Influenza, the Last Great Plague: An Unfinished Story of Discovery* (New York: Prodist, 1978).

Hoehling, A.A. *The Great Epidemic* (Boston: Little, Brown, 1961).

Katz, Robert S. "Influenza 1918–1919: A Study in Mortality." *Bulletin of the History of Medicine* 48 (Fall 1974): 416–22.

Prisoners of War (POWs) and Internees

At the end of WWI there were more than 6.5 million POWs being held in Europe alone. During the war some POWs were conscripted or allowed to volunteer for military service in the opposing forces; German POWs in France who were Polish were allowed to enlist in the Polish army in France. Some Russian POWs in German camps were used as labor on the Hindenburg Line. A condition identified by the Swiss called *stacheldrahtkrankheit*, or barbed-wire disease, was commonly found in all camps. The symptoms were lethargy, inability to concentrate, and outbreaks of hostility. Those who were able to work or develop pastimes fared better than the others.

After the Armistice, some prisoners held in Russia were not repatriated with the other POWs. Many had to walk home, and some were conscripted to fight in the Russian Civil War. The American Red Cross estimated that as late as 1924 there were still 6,773 POWs left in Russia.[16]

International Red Cross, Geneva, Switzerland

International Prisoner of War Agency
- Lists of all WWI POWs and internees of all nationalities
- Deaths in POW camps
- Records of POW exchanges and repatriation
- Interviews with POWs regarding others reported missing in action

Most of the Red Cross societies that participated in WWI were: American Red Cross, British Red Cross Society, Danish Red Cross, German Red Cross, Japanese Red Cross, Norwegian Red Cross, Polish White Cross, Russian Red Cross, Swedish Red Cross, and the Turkish Red Crescent Society. The national headquarters of each country has records for prisoners and casualties of war.

International Committee of the Red Cross
Documentation and Library Service
19 avenue de la Paix
1202 Geneva

National Archives, Washington, DC

Records of the American Expeditionary Force (**RG 120**)
- Casualty Information and Check Station name file of men reported missing in action or POWs, 1918 (RG 120.4.1)

---

[16] Samuel R. Williamson and Peter Pastor, *Essays on World War I: Origins and Prisoners of War* (New York: Social Science Monographs, Brooklyn College Press, 1983), 255.

- Central Records Office correspondence and lists relating to American POWs in Germany (RG 120.4.1)
- Central Records Office correspondence and lists relating to German and Austro-Hungarian POWs held by the AEF, 1918–19 (RG 120.4.1)
- Prisoner of war labor companies, 1918–19 (RG 120.7.4)
- Permanent International Armistice Commission (PIAC) for repatriating Allied civilians and POWs, Belgian, British, and French correspondence, 1918–20 (RG 120.14.6)
- PIAC correspondence of American troop detachments at POW camps concerning Russian war prisoners and war prisoner repatriation, 1919 (RG 120.14.6)
- PIAC records of the U.S. Military Mission to Berlin, 1919 (RG 120.14.6)

Records of the Adjutant General's Office (**RG 407**)

- Disciplinary and internment camps at Fort McPherson and Fort Oglethorpe in Georgia, Fort Douglas, Utah, and Governor's Island, New York (RG 407.4.4)
- Case files of POWs and imprisoned enemy aliens, 1917–19 (RG 407.4.4)
- Applications for citizenship, enemy POWs (RG 407.79.28)

Records of the Immigration and Naturalization Service (**RG 85**)

- Records of WWI internment camps for enemy aliens, Hot Springs, North Carolina, 1917–19 (RG 85.4.1)

Camps Douglas and Oglethorpe were for "Enemy Aliens," Fort McPherson held German naval personnel. Camp Douglas also held naval POWs for a short time. Of the Fort McPherson POWs, some 600 were sent to work in camps in Illinois, Massachusetts, Ohio, and South Carolina.

Public Record Office (PRO), Kew, Surrey (England)

Many records were destroyed in a bombing raid in 1940.

British and Dominion POWs in Germany, Turkey, and Switzerland, 1916 (**AIR 1/892/204/5/696–8**)

Army POWS in Germany, July 1915 (**ADM 1/8420/124**)

Deaths of POWs and internees, military and non-military hospitals in enemy and occupied territory (**RG 35**)

Interviews with returned POWs (**WO 161/95–101**)

Specimens of classes of documents destroyed (1940) relating to POWs, 1914–18 (**WO 900**)

Imperial War Museum, London

Germany and German-occupied territories: Imperial POWs, alphabetical list (compiled 1944) gives camp, POW number, army number, and name of regiment or corps

- British Army
- Australian Imperial Force
- Canadian Expeditionary Force
- 2nd New Zealand Expeditionary Force
- South African Union Defence Forces
- Indian army
- Naval forces
- Air forces
- Merchant Navy
- Miscellaneous, including Palestinians and Cypriots
- POWs in Italy

Kriegsarchiv, Vienna, Austria
- POW card index, 1914–18

Australian National Archives, Canberra
- 4th Military District, South Australia, photograph album of internees, 1914–18 (**D3597**)
- 6th Military District, Tasmania, record of POWs, 1914–16 (**A405**)
- Governor-General's Office, correspondence relating to WWI POWs (**CP 78/23/4**)
- German Red Cross inquiries about Germans in Australia, 1920 (**A390**)

South Australia Office of the Australian Archives, Collinswood
- Deported aliens, lists by name and ship, 1914–46 (**D1918**)
- 4th Military District, Torrens Island Camp nominal rolls of internees, 1914–19 (**D2286**)
- 4th Military District index cards to POWs, 1914–19 (**D23375**)

Kizil Ay (Red Crescent Society), Ankara, Turkey
The Society holds extensive records on Ottoman POWs in Allied hands and Allied POWs interned by the Ottoman Empire.

Hoover Institution, Stanford University, Stanford, California
Materials and manuscripts relating to:
- British POWs, Ruhleben POW Camp, Germany
- Austrian POWs in Siberia
- Allied POWs in Austria
- American and British POWs in Russia during the Russian Civil War
- Estonian POWs in Germany
- Belgians deported to Germany
- Hungarian POWs in Russia

- Russian POWs in Germany
POW newsletters:
- Altengrabow POW Camp, Germany, Russian POW newsletters
- Crefeld POW Camp, Germany, British and American POW newsletters
- Camp Oglethorpe, Georgia (U.S.), German POW newsletters

Further Reading

Batzler-Heim, G. *Horrors of Cayenne: The Experiences of a German as a French Bagno-Convict* (London: Constable, 1933).

Burdick, Charles and Ursula Moessner. *The German Prisoners of War in Japan, 1914-1920* (London: Lanham, 1984).

Cohen-Portheim, P. *Time Stood Still: My Internment in England, 1914-1918* (London: Duckworth, 1931).

Davison, Henry P. *The American Red Cross in the Great War* (New York: Macmillan, 1920).

Dennet, Carl P. *Prisoners of the Great War* (Boston: Houghton Mifflin, 1919).

Epstein, Berly and Sam Eppstein. *The Story of the International Red Cross* (New York: Thomas Nelson and Sons, 1963).

Fischer, Gerhard. *Enemy Aliens: Internment and the American Homefront Experience in Australia, 1914-1920* (Saint Lucia: University of Queensland Press, 1989).

Forder, A. *In Brigands' Hands and Turkish Prisons, 1914-1918* (London: Marshall, 1920).

Glidden, William B. "Internment Camps in America, 1917-1920." *Military Affairs* 37 (December 1973): 137-41.

Harvey, F.W. *Comrades in Captivity: A Record of Life in Seven German Prison Camps* (London: Sigwick and Jackson, 1920).

Hauser, K. *Swiss Internment of POWs* (New York: Columbia University Press, 1917).

Jackson, Robert. *The Prisoners, 1914-1918* (London: Routledge Ltd,, 1989).

Moynihan, Michael. *Black Bread and Barbed Wire: Prisoners of the First World War* (London: Leo Cooper, 1978).

Picot, H.P. *The British Interned in Switzerland* (London: Arnold, 1919).

Williamson, Samuel R. and Peter Pastor. *Essays on World War I: Origins and Prisoners of War* (New York: Social Science Monographs, 1983).

> Today there are no prisons for the crews of the merchantmen, but they can go to the bottom by mine and torpedo even more quickly than their ancestors were run into Le Havre. The submarine takes the place of the privateer; the line, as in old days, is occupied bombarding and blockading elsewhere, but the seaborne traffic must continue, and that is being looked after by the lineal descendants of the crews of the long extinct cutters and sloops and gun brigs.
>
> — Rudyard Kipling, from *With the British Fleet*

Major Political Changes of States, Provinces, and Nations after World War I		
1914	**Country**	**End of WWI**
Alsace-Lorraine (Elaß-Lothringen)	German Empire	France, Department of Alsace, Lothringia in French Department of Moselle
Banat, Hungary	Austro-Hungarian Empire	Yugoslavia
Belarus (Belorussia)	Russian Empire	Republic of Poland/ USSR
Bessarabia	Russian Empire	Romania
Bohemia, Austria	Austro-Hungarian Empire	Czechoslovakia
Bosnia	Austro-Hungarian Empire	Yugoslavia
Bukovina, Austria	Austro-Hungarian Empire	Romania
Bulgaria	Bulgaria	size reduced by territory ceded to Greece, Romania, and Yugoslavia
Burgenland, Hungary	Austro-Hungarian Empire	Austria
Carinthia, Austria	Austro-Hungarian Empire	Italy/Yugoslavia
Coburg, of Sachsen-Coburg-Gotha, Sachsen	German Empire	Bavaria, Germany
Croatia, Hungary	Austro-Hungarian Empire	Yugoslavia
Dalmatia, Hungary	Austro-Hungarian Empire	Yugoslavia
Danzig, West Prussia, Prussia	German Empire	Free City of Danzig

Major Political Changes of States, Provinces, and Nations after World War I		
1914	**Country**	**End of WWI**
East Prussia, Prussia	German Empire	Germany /Lithuania (north)
Estonia	Russian Empire	Independent State of Estonia
Eupen and Malmédy districts, Rhineland, Prussia	German Empire	Belgium
Finland	Russian Empire	Independent State of Finland
Fiume, Austria	Austro-Hungarian Empire	Free City of Fiume
Galicia (West), Austria	Austro-Hungarian Empire	Republic of Poland
Galicia (East), Austria	Austro-Hungarian Empire	protectorate of the Republic of Poland
Gorizia	Italy	Italy/Yugoslavia
Herzegovina	Austro-Hungarian Empire	Yugoslavia
Hungary	Austro-Hungarian Empire	retains one-third of original size; cedes territory to Austria, Czechoslovakia, Romania, and Yugoslavia
Istria, Austria	Austro-Hungarian Empire	Italy
Jutland, Schleswig-Holstein, Prussia	German Empire	Denmark
Latvia	Russian Empire	Independent State of Latvia

Major Political Changes of States, Provinces, and Nations after World War I		
1914	**Country**	**End of WWI**
Lithuania	Russian Empire	Independent State of Lithuania
Macedonia	Serbia	Yugoslavia
Montenegro, Hungary	Austro-Hungarian Empire	Yugoslavia
Moravia, Austria	Austro-Hungarian Empire	Czechoslovakia
Poland	Russian Empire	Republic of Poland
Posen	German Empire	Germany/Republic of Poland
Russia	Russian Empire	USSR; some territory ceded to Romania and Poland; Baltic States and Finland become independent
Ruthenia, Hungary	Austro-Hungarian Empire	Czechoslovakia
Saarland	German Empire	League of Nations (until 1935)
Sachsen (Saxony)	German Empire	State of Thuringia, Germany
Serbia (independent kingdom), Hungary	Austro-Hungarian Empire	Yugoslavia
Silesia, Austria / Germany	Austro-Hungarian Empire/ German Empire	Czechoslovakia/ Poland (Upper Silesia)
Slavonia, Hungary	Austro-Hungarian Empire	Yugoslavia/Romania
Slovakia, Hungary	Austro-Hungarian Empire	Czechoslovakia

Major Political Changes of States, Provinces, and Nations after World War I		
1914	Country	End of WWI
Slovenia, Austria	Austro-Hungarian Empire	Yugoslavia
Styria, Austria	Austro-Hungarian Empire	Italy/Yugoslavia
Transylvania, Hungary	Austro-Hungarian Empire	Romania
Trieste	Italy	Italy/Yugoslavia
Turkey	Ottoman Empire	Turkish Republic; size reduced by territory ceded to Greece and Italy
Tyrol, Austria	Austro-Hungarian Empire	Austria (north)/ Italy (south)
Ukraine	Russian Empire / Austro-Hungarian Empire	Republic of Poland/ USSR
West Prussia, Prussia	German Empire	Germany/Republic of Poland

Gazetteers

Allgemeines Verzeichnis der Ortsgemeinden und Ortschaften Österreichs: Nach den Ergebnissen der Volkszählung vom 31. Dezember 1910 (Vienna: Verlag der k.k. Hof-und Staatsdruckerei, 1915, film 1186712). Gazetteer of the Austrian Empire, based on the 1910 census. Covers Austria and parts of Czechoslovakia, Poland, Yugoslavia, and Ukraine.

Gemeindelexikon der im Reichsrathe vertretenen Königreiche und Länder: Bearbeitet auf Grund der Ergebnisse der Volkszählung vom 31. Dezember 1900. 14 Vols. (Vienna: Verlag der k.k. Hof-und Staatsdruckerei, 1905–8, film 1187925). Gazetteers of each of the states of the Austrian Empire:

Niederösterreich	Krain	Mähren
Oberösterreich	Küstenland	Galizien
Salzburg	Tirol und Vorarlberg	Bukowina
Steiermark	Böhmen	Dalmatien
KФarnten	Schlesien	

Koturović, Stev M. *Recnik mesta u kraljevini srbiji* (Belgrade: n.p., 1892, film 1256330). Gazetteer of the Kingdom of Serbia.

Kredel, Otto. *Deutsch-fremdsprachiges Ortsnamenverzeichnis* (Berlin: Deutsche Verlagsgesellschaft, 1931, film 0583457). Dictionary of place-name changes following WWI showing German place-names assigned to the following countries: Belgium, Czechoslovakia, Denmark, Estonia, France, Hungary, Italy, Latvia, Lithuania, Luxembourg, Poland, Romania, Russia, Switzerland, and Yugoslavia.

Mayerhofer, Hans. *Österreich-ungarisches orts-lxikon enthaltend die pfarrorte, cultusgemeinden und filialen aller confessionen: Österreich-Ungarns, Bosniens, und der Herzegowina* (Vienna: Carl Fromme, 1896, film 1256324). Gazetteer of the Austro-Hungarian Empire showing all parishes and church jurisdictions.

Ortsverzeichnis zur Gemeindekarte von Rumänien (Vienna: Publikationsstelle Wien, 1940, film 0583460). Gazetteer of Romania, with the former Bulgarian, Russian, and German names of cities now in Romania.

Regényi, Isabella, et al. *Donauschwäbisches Ortsnamenbuch: für die ehemals und teilweise noch deutsch besiedelten Orte in Ungarn, Jugoslawien [ohne Slowenien] sowie West-Rumäien [Banat und Sathmar]* (Schriesheim: Arbeitskreis donauschwäbischer Familienforscher, 1987). Gazetteer of place-names for former German colonies in Hungary, Yugoslavia (excluding Slovenia), and West Romania (the Banat and Satmar regions). Includes equivalent names in German, Hungarian, Romanian, and Serbo-Croatian.

A magyar szent korona országainak helységnévtára, 1913 (Budapest: Pesti Könyvnyomda Rt., 1913). Gazetteer of Hungary, 1913, divided into sections for Hungary and for Horvát-Szlavonországok, later known as the region of Slavonia in Croatia.

Magyarország helységnévtára, 1944 (Budapest: Hornyánszky Ny., 1944, fiche 6053520). Gazetteer of Hungary, 1944, including territories formerly part of the Empire that were regained temporarily during World War II. The last section contains an alphabetical list of localities in Austria, Slovakia, Transylvania, and Yugoslavia (part of the former Empire but not regained during the war) with the variant spellings of the place-names in the languages by which they were known.

17 Gaston M. Bigot, French army, killed at Menastir, Greek Macedonia
(Liberty Memorial Museum)

Part Four

APPENDIX

I know that I shall meet my fate
Somewhere among the clouds above,
Those that I fight I do not hate,
Those that I guard I do not love . . .
— William Butler Yeats,
An Irish Airman Forsees His Death

18 German commemoration ribbons (U.S. Naval Historical Center)

Sources on the Internet

European National Libraries
portico.bl.uk/gabriel/en/eurocoun.html

The web site *Gabriel: Gateway to Europe's National Libraries* provides links to home pages of many national libraries. The information given varies from only basic information (address, phone, hours), to some detail about collections and holdings. Some sites are in English, some are only in the native language. Countries included that are relevant to this book are: Albania, Austria, Belgium, Bulgaria, Czech Republic, Estonia, Finland, France, Germany, Greece, Hungary, Ireland, Italy, Latvia, Lithuania, Luxembourg, Macedonia, Poland, Portugal, Romania, Russia, Slovakia, Slovenia, Turkey, and the U.K. (the British Library).

Australian Archives
www.aa.gov.au/AA_WWW/AA_Sect_Serv/AA_WW1/AA_WW1.html
World War I records

National Archives of Canada
www.archives.ca/db/cef/records.html

The National Archives maintains a web site on the records of the Canadian Expeditionary Force (CEF), including a searchable database of CEF members.

Information Resource Centre, Canadian Forces College, Department of National Defence
www.cfsc.dnd.ca/links/milhist/index.html

Public Record Office (PRO), U.K.
www.open.gov.uk/pro/prohome.htm

The home page of the PRO has many features, including information about WWI service records. A series of *PRO Information Leaflets* can be printed or downloaded, including:

➢ No. 6 *Operational Records of the British Army in the First World War*
➢ No. 13 *Air Records as Sources for Biography and Family History*
➢ No. 49 *Operational Records of the Royal Navy, 1914–1919*
➢ No. 74 *Royal Marines Records*
➢ No. 101 *Service Medal and Award Rolls War of 1914–1918*
➢ No. 105 *Indexes to British Army First World War Medal Entitlement*

Archives in Russia
www.iisg.nl/~abb/

The *ArcheoBiblioBase* is an information system on archival repositories in the Russian Federation. This was published as *Archives in Russia: A Directory and Bibliography Guide to the Holdings in Moscow and Saint Petersburg* (Moscow: Arkheograficheskii tsentr, 1997) and will be published in the U.S. by M.E. Sharpe sometime in 1998. The on-line information is basically bibliographical.

www.den.davis.ca/us/go/feefhs/blitz/frgblitz.html

BLITZ Russian-Baltic Information Center, Saint Petersburg/San Rafael, CA

National Archives and Records Administration (U.S.)
www.nara.gov

Military service records, microfilm catalog

www.nara.gov/genealogy/holdings/catalogs/ipcat/ipcat.html

National Personnel Records Center

gopher.nara.gov/nara/frc/mpromp.html

Military Historical Libraries (U.S.)
www.army.mil/cmh-pg/musdir.htm

directory of U.S. Army museums

www.army.mil/cmh-pg/records.htm

master index of U.S. Army records

www.army.mil/cmh-pg

Center of Military History, Washington, DC

carlisle-www.army.mil/usamhi/

Military History Institute, Carlisle Barracks, Pennsylvania

www.history.navy.mil

Navy Historical Center, Washington, DC

www.usmc.mil/wwwmain/hist.htm

Marine Corps Historical Center, Washington, DC

www.history.navy.mil/branches/nhcorg7.htm

Navy Department Library, Washington, DC

www.dot.gov/dotinfo/uscg/h_biblio/h_bibdx.html

Coast Guard Historian's Office, Washington, DC

www.gcmarshallfdn.org/archives.html

George C. Marshall Library and Archives, Virginia Military Institute, Lexington

Library of Congress (U.S.)
lcweb.loc.gov/

Hoover Institution Archives, Stanford University
www-hoover.stanford.edu

New York Public Library, New York, New York
www.nypl.org/research/chss/subguides/milhist/wwinypl.html
World War I resources in the NYPL

New Zealand National Archives, Wellington
www.archives.dia.govt.nz

It is a disturbing thought, to wonder now, and even think of men who yearn for understanding, passing by. They had to live alone, and sometimes die, because of selfishness. But then, you cannot let many people get inside. A fellow does not know 'til afterward that little pieces of his heart will rot in the graves where friends are fast asleep.

—Elton E. Mackin, from *Suddenly We Didn't Want to Die*

19 U.S. Army sentinel on guard in France (National Archives)

Glossary and Abbreviations

ABMC. American Battle Monuments Commission

ACF. Active Citizen Force (South Africa)

AEF. American Expeditionary Force

Aid post. Nearest medical post to firing line

AIF. Australian Imperial Force

AIR. Air Historical Branch (U.K.)

ALH. Australian Light Horse

Allied Powers. The alliance of Belgium, Brazil, France, Great Britain (and dominions of the British Empire), Greece, Italy, Japan, Montenegro, Portugal, Romania, the Russian Empire, Serbia, and the U.S. in WWI; aka *Entente Cordiale*

ANZAC. Australia-New Zealand Army Corps

archie. Anti-aircraft fire

ARS. *Appareil respiratoire speciale*, French gas mask

askaris. Native colonial troops from Africa

AWM. Australian War Memorial

AWOL. Absent Without Official Leave (U.S.)

BA-MA. *Bundesarchiv Abteilung Militärarchiv* (Germany)

BEF. British Expeditionary Force

BKdo. *Bezirkskommando* (German recruiting district)

BLITZ. Russian Baltic Information Center

CA. *Corps d'armee* (French Army Corps)

casualties. Those killed, wounded, or missing in action

CEF. Canadian Expeditionary Force

Central Powers. The alliance of Austria-Hungary, Bulgaria, Germany, and Turkey in WWI

CEP. Portuguese Expeditionary Force

CO. Commanding officer

cossack. Heavy cavalry units (Russian)

CP. Collecting post, a location used to collect wounded or prisoners

CT. Communications trench

DOW. Dead of Wounds

Dreadnought. Class of British battleship

Družina. Czech Legion

EEF. Egyptian Expeditionary Force

Entente Cordiale. See Allied Powers

FF. Field punishment, non-judicial

FHL. Family History Library

FHLC. Family History Library Catalog

FOO. Forward Observation Officer

Fritz. Slang for a German soldier

front. Used to designate a theater of operations: western, eastern, Balkan, Italian, Middle Eastern

fusilier. Infantry regiment (British and German)

GHQ. General Headquarters

Gotha. Name associated with all large German bombers

grenadier. Infantry regiment (German)

GRO. General Registry Office (Scotland)

GRS. Graves Registration Service (U.S.)

GS. General Service

GSO. General Staff Officer

HE. High explosive

HKK. *Höheren Kavallerie-Kommandeure* (German cavalry)

Hochseeflotte. High Seas Fleet (German)

Honvéd. Hungarian territorial army

Hun. Slang for a German soldier

hussar. Heavy cavalry regiment (German)

jäger. German rifleman

KIA. Killed in Action

krieg. War (German)

kriegsgefallene. War casualties (German)

KuK. *Kaiserlich und Königlich*, Austro-Hungarian army

Landwehr. Territorial army in Austria, Germany

LI. Light infantry

light horse. Mounted infantry

LP. Listening Post

MO. Medical Officer

MOD. Ministry of Defence (U.K.)

narodna vojska. Serbian territorial army

narodon opolchie. Bulgarian territorial army

Nizam. Turkish army

NYD. Not Yet Diagnosed, slang: "not yet dead," and "no, you don't."

NZEF. New Zealand Expeditionary Force

ONI. Office of Naval Intelligence (U.S.)

ONS. Office of National Statistics (U.K.)

over the top. To climb out of the trench and attack

panzer. Tank (German)

PC. *Poste de command*, French command post

PIAC. Permanent International Armistice Commission

PMG. Paymaster General (U.K.)

POW. Prisoner of War

PRO. Public Record Office (U.K.)

Q-ship. Decoy ship (British)

RAAF. Royal Australian Air Force

RAF. Royal Air Force (U.K.)

RAGAS. Russian-American Genealogical Archival Service

ratniki opolcheniia. Russian territorial militia

RE. Royal Engineers (U.K.)

RFC. Royal Flying Corps (U.K.)

RG. Record group (U.S.)

RGAVMF. Russian State Archive of the Navy

RGVA. Russian State Military Archive

RGVIA. Russian State Military Historical Archive

RM. Royal Marines (U.K.)

RMA. Royal Marine Artillery (U.K.)

RMLE. *Régiment du Marche* (French)

RMLI. Royal Marine Light Infantry (U.K.)

RN. Royal Navy (U.K.)

RNAS. Royal Naval Air Service (U.K.)

SAFA. South African Field Artillery

STAVKA. Russian Imperial Army Headquarters

Sturmtruppen. Storm troops (German)

Tirallieur. A colonial regiment in the French army

Tommy. Slang for British soldier

U-boat. *Unterseeboote,* German submarine

uhlans. Elite light cavalry (German and Russian)

UK. United Kingdom

USMC. United States Marine Corps

VA. Veterans' Administration, now Department of Veterans' Affairs (U.S.)

WIA. Wounded in Action

WO. War Office (U.K.)

WPA. Works Progress (later Work Projects) Administration (U.S.)

WWI. World War One

YMCA. Young Men's Christian Association, also the "Y" (U.S.)

Z. Zero hour, time when an attack started

20 Ferdinand Klutz, German Imperial Army (property of Barry C. Fox)

Selected Bibliography of Books in English

Bayliss, Gwyn M. *Bibliographic Guide to the Two World Wars: An Annotated Survey of English-Language Reference Materials* (New York: Bowker Publishing Ltd, 1977).

Bishop, James. *The Illustrated London New Social History of the First World War* (London: Angus & Robertson, 1982).

Burdick, Charles B. "Foreign Military Records of World War I in the National Archives." *Prologue* 7 (Winter 1975): 213–20.

Churchill, Winston S. *The Aftermath* (New York: Charles Scribner's Sons, 1929).

Coombs, Rose E.B. *Before Endeavours Fade: A Guide to the Battlefields of the First World War* (London: After the Battle, 1983).

Cruttwell, C.R.M.F. *A History of the Great War, 1914–1918* (Oxford: Clarendon Press, 1964).

Enser, A.G.S. *A Subject Bibliography of the First World War: Books in English, 1914–1978* (London: Andre Deutsch, 1979).

Falls, Cyril. *The Great War, 1914–1918* (New York: Capricorn Books, 1961).

Gilbert, Martin. *The First World War: A Complete History* (London: Oxford University Press, 1970)

Gray, Randal. *Chronicle of the First World War.* 2 Vols. (New York: Facts on File, 1990). Day-by-day record of events from July 1914 to the formal termination of hostilities in August 1921.

Halpern, Paul. *A Naval History of World War I* (Annapolis, MD: Naval Institute Press, 1993).

Haythornthwaite Philip J. *The World War One Source Book* (London: Arms and Armour, 1992).

Heyman, Neil M. *World War I* (Westport, CT: Greenwood Press, 1997).

Horne, Charles F. *Source Records of the Great War*. 7 Vols. (Indianapolis: The American Legion, 1931).

Jane's Fighting Aircraft of World War I (London: Military Press, 1990).

Jane's Fighting Ships of World War I (London: Military Press, 1990).

Jelavich, Charles. *The Establishment of the Balkan National States, 1804–1920* (Seattle: University of Washington Press, 1977). Covers Albania, Bulgaria, Greece, Hungary, Romania, and Yugoslavia.

The Marshall Cavendish Encyclopedia of World War I. 12 Vols. (New York: M. Cavendish, 1984).

Mayer, Sydney L. *The Two World Wars: A Guide to Manuscript Collections in the United Kingdom* (London: Bower, 1976).

New York Public Library. *Subject Catalog of the World War I Collections*. 4 Vols. (Boston: G.K. Hall, 1961).

Pope, Stephen and Elizabeth-Anne Wheal. *The Dictionary of the First World War* (New York: St. Martin's Press, 1995).

Randall, Gray. *Chronicle of the First World War*. 2 Vols. (New York: Facts on File, 1991).

Taylor, A.J.P. *History of World War One* (London: Octopus Books, 1972).

Tuchman, Barbara W. *The Guns of August* (New York: Macmillan, 1962).

Tucker, Spencer C. *The European Powers in the First World War: An Encyclopedia* (New York: Garland, 1996).

Vansittart, Peter. *Voices from the Great War* (New York: Franklin Watts, 1984).

Warships and Sea Battles of World War I (New York: Beekman House, 1993).

Winter, Jay and Blaine Winter. *The Great War and the Shaping of the Twentieth Century* (New York: Penguin Studio, 1996).

Wren, Jack. *The Great Battles of World War One* (New York: Castle Books, 1971).

Index